AF322988

KISS
AT 50

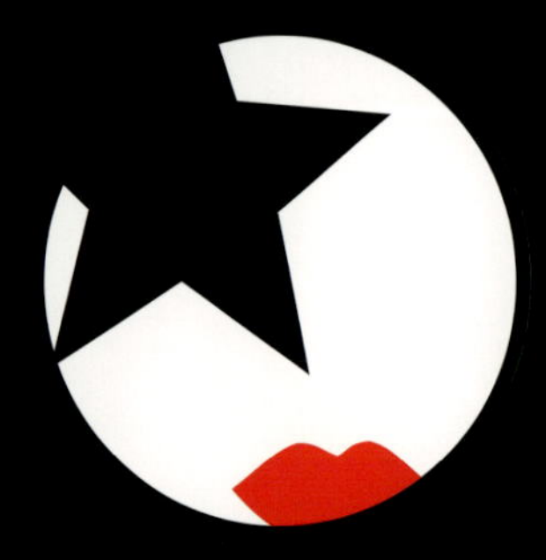

KISS
AT 50

CONTENTS

ALL WORLD TOUR
1977~1978
KISS
STAGE CREW
1-20-78
KISS
THE FAREWELL TOUR
WORKING
DETROIT TV

KISS
WORKING / STAGEHAND
ALIVE/
WORLDWIDE
'96~'97
TIGER STADIUM

COBO ARENA · JAN. 27, 1976
KISS
steve glantz productions
DETROIT - 3rd SHOW

BELKIN PRODUCTIONS
KISS
TOLEDO 7-31-76

INTRODUCTION

Like a smoke 'n' leather gift to the '70s, Kiss were always there, raising a pile of us kids of that generation, not only me an' my buds, but a Kiss Army of friends I now have all over the world that I've met through the process of writing rock books and doing video and podcast stuff online.

Surely, sometimes Paul, Gene, Ace, and Peter were banished to the back of kid consciousness—in the corner and with a dunce cap—but they were always garishly present, always the companion band, and in fact actually from the beginning—Kiss are indeed distinguished in my memory banks as the first band I was onboard with for every album since their debut release, tied with Rush, both debuting in 1974 when I was eleven. So yes, blessing this book with neatness, I discovered Kiss exactly when the first record came out. *Kiss*, as it was authoritatively called, just showed up one day on the racks at either Kelly's or Rock Island Tape Centre or Koo's TV or Little John's—usually all within a few days of each other—in downtown Trail, BC, population twelve thousand (now nine thousand). But as an important distinction, it was Forrest Toop who bought it, so for the time being, he was the main Kiss guy, the Kiss boss of Trail.

Kiss would have invaded the available mind-sphere for such matters among my group of friends in grade six, which is neither here nor there because there's no connection between Kiss and school for me. The main point is when Kiss arrived, pressed on a questionable but zesty and purple label named Casablanca, our gang of banana-seat kids already knew about heavy metal. I wasn't on the ball enough to know the first record was coming before it arrived, but give it twelve more months, with the discovery

of *Circus, Creem,* and *Hit Parader* (possibly even *Rock Scene*), and me an' the buds were little, angry hard-rock experts by that point, some of us set up for years of pretty intense fandom. The point is, *Hotter Than Hell* was anticipated, as was *Dressed to Kill,* which I have extra fondness for because that was the first Kiss album that I was the first among my friend set to get. This made me the "presenter" of the product, showcasing it for the visiting inspectors with the foreknowledge of what happens after the pretty acoustic music at the beginning of "Rock Bottom".

But that's not my fondest memory.

Apologies if you've heard this story before (perhaps on some YouTube show or radio interview I did), but one day Forrest and I are rummaging around the town garbage dump, a storied pastime for kids in Trail back in the day. We had barely gotten halfway up the yellow sand road toward the main garbage heaps and there it was on the side of the road: an open, pristine cardboard box filled with a mint 2-inch (5 cm) stack of April Wine 1974 tour posters, themed on that crazy, evil-looking black-and-purple front cover to the April Wine *Live* album. Jackpot!

I had a school dance planned in my basement coming up in a few days. My dad, the industrial education teacher at the high school in Rossland, was always building cool things, and one that would come in handy for the dance was what we called a light organ. This was a tower of colored lights in a wood case, fronted by patterned plastic, with a single speaker wire coming out the back that you spliced into the speaker wire coming from the amp to your speakers. The different frequencies would set off different colored lights, so bass would give you red, green would give you midrange, blue might give you treble, and so forth. The pattern turned the lights into doughnut shapes. I had a couple 18" (45 cm) ones too, plus a couple strobes.

This, of course, would look better if we took every one of those black-and-purple April Wine posters and taped them up floor to ceiling all the way around all four walls of the basement rec room, plus door, cutting around for light switches and plugs, which is what we did. We have the dance straight after school, beginning about four in the afternoon, and there are about seven girls and seven guys. I distinctly remember one of the girlie songs being on: Elton John's "Crocodile Rock." Everybody's up there dancing, all the guys are totally hating it, and in bursts Bobby Davidson, a brand-new, shrink-wrapped copy of *Alive!* held high in the air.

KISS
LICK IT UP

KISS
CARNIVAL OF SOULS
THE FINAL SESSIONS

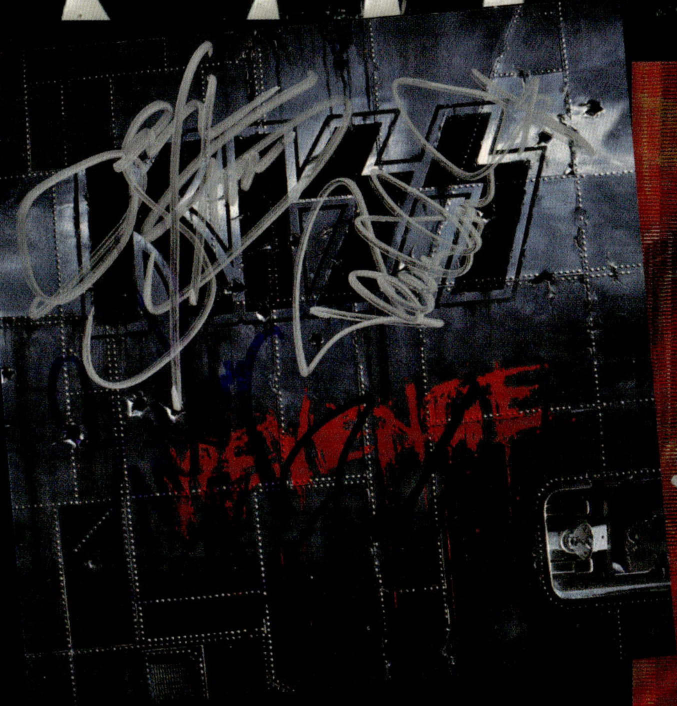

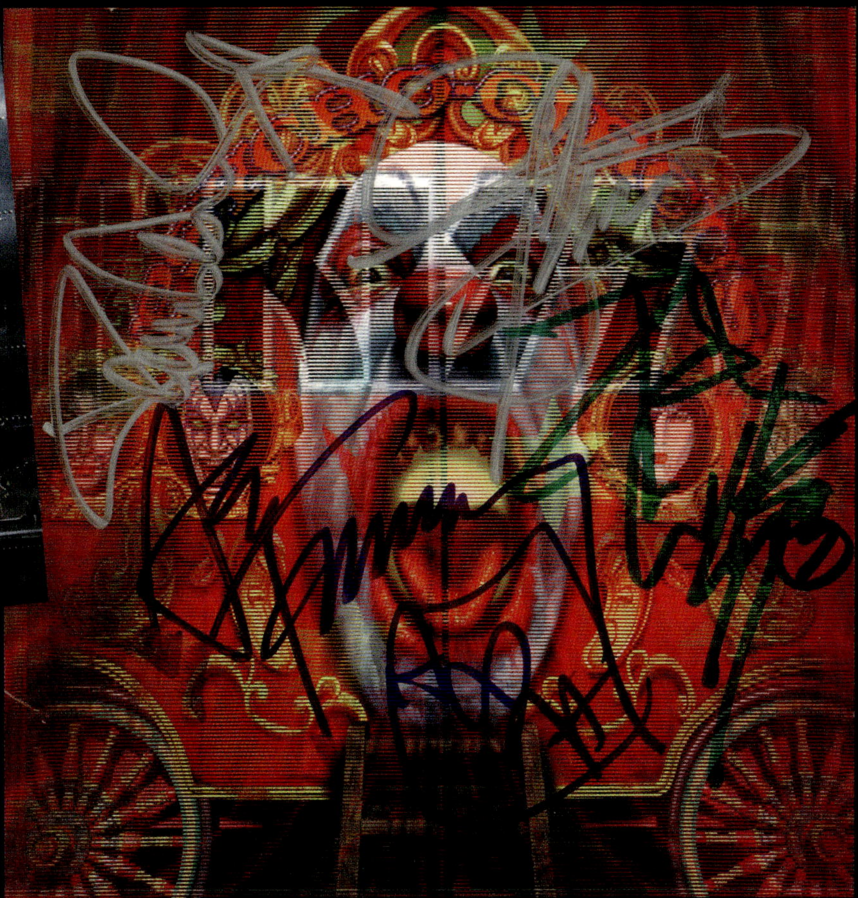

75¢
JULY 1976
HIT PARADER
CHARLTON
CDC 00045
PUBLICATION
KISS
MORE MALICE
THAN ALICE?
QUEEN
TECHNOFLASH
WIZARDS STAGE
A POP OPERA
ROBERT PLANT
EXCLUSIVE INTERVIEW
"TIME IS THE TEACHER....
I'VE BEEN THE PUPIL"
BAD COMPANY
AHEAD OF THE PACK
BILL WYMAN
STONE ROLLS ALONE
DAVID BOWIE
STARK ROCK IN BLACK AND WHITE
RON WOOD
HAS GUITAR, WILL TRAVEL
WORDS TO
LATEST HIT
0 0987654321
QUEEN • RINGO • STARZ • PATTI SMITH • CLAPTON
$1.00
02137
America's Only Rock 'n' Roll Magazine
JANUARY 1977
50p
CREEM
FRAMPTON
The Inside Story
NUGENT
Madman Backs Down!
INTERVIEW:
HALL & OATES
Expose Themselves!
ZEP MOVIE
Worth The Wait?
FASHION WRAP-UP:
Who Wore What In '76
BOWIE vs. SLICK
BOSTON Breaks
MONTROSE Macho
Thin Lizzy • Seger
Lou Reed • More!
KISS TALKS!
Bat Lizard & Pirate Dog
Reveal Unearthly
Utterances!
BONUS!
MERRY KISSMAS POSTER
AND OTHER GOODIES!
0 71486 02137
CIRCUS — THE LEADING ROCK & ROLL BI-WEEKLY
ISSUE NO. 130   APRIL 8, 1975
TRUE STORY: THE WORLD'S NO. 1 PRIVA
EXCLUSIVE: BETTE MIDLER ON BETTE M
EVERY TWO WEEKS
CIRCUS
KISS
SPECIAL REPORT
On Rock's New
Superheroes
THEIR
MASTERPLAN To
Dominate The '70s
'DESTROYER'
How They Made It,
How It Will Make
Them
BAD CO.
The Platinum
Pack Is Back
DOOBIES
SKUNK BAXTER
Interview
QUEEN
Britain's Hottest
New Band
Brings 'Opera'
To America
SQUIRE
Yes's Romantic
Bassist Goes
Solo
TOURS
Kiss, Bad Co
ELO, Johnny Winter,
Sweet, Bowie
CONVOY
The Ad-man
Who Became
A Truckstop Hero
PLUS: A Glossary Of
Highway Slang
PURPLE
Lord, Coverdale &
Hughes Announce
Solo LPs
TULL
Announce
New Bassist
HEEP
The Story Behind
Gary Thain's Death.

Gene Simmons, Martin Popoff, Paul Stanley, Tommy Thayer, and Eric Singer at the *Monster* release party, September 14, 2012, at Noble Studios in Toronto, Ontario.

I can picture what followed next as clear as the day it happened. All the guys immediately stopped dancing and dog-piled on Bobby, with his arm extended as he was tackled to the floor so that the record wouldn't get bent. One of us wrenched it out of his hand and tore the shrink-wrap off, and what ensued was a quiet and intense listening party as we perused every morsel of the packaging.

Eventually we looked up and all the girls had left—end of dance.

Fast-forward through the decades and there's a Kiss album set against every trend in the music industry and accompanying every personal and career milestone in my life. This leads up to a late-period highlight where I got invited to an industry release party for the *Monster* album and I got to meet all the guys, get pictures taken, get a few things signed, putting a big red bow on this whole life with Kiss, first album to the last.

In any event, thank you for indulging a few personal memories, but I should probably offer a few missives on the project at hand. I can't take credit for the concept of *Kiss @ 50*. This fetching idea came from the publisher. They've indeed got other books going in this series, and in fact I did one last year called *Bowie @ 75*. The concept is simply this: Kiss have now been around for fifty years, and we are marking those fifty years by celebrating fifty career highlights along the way. Each of these entries might not, strictly speaking, represent a happy highlight. Some of them are more like milestones or major news events. But the idea is that these are fifty big things that happened to the band along the way. Fortunately for me, I get to write about them in this, the first Kiss book I've ever done despite being about 120 titles into this life as a paid fanboy.

I've also put together five sidebars, which I themed stylistically as interview-material intensive, even if I couldn't resist dovetailing in a few extra quotes along the way within some of the regular entries. My editor, Dennis Pernu, and the insanely talented Motorbooks graphics team took over from there, turning *Kiss @ 50* into a gorgeously appointed celebration of this band I've loved for every one of those fifty years of their charmed existence. I hope that admiration resonates (and is something you share as well) as you peruse the following hotter-than-hell pages, culminating in my thoughts on the tour that Paul and Gene have indicated (for sure, this time) marks the band's final farewell.

PART ONE
KISS MAJOR

Kiss perform on the second of two nights at the Hammersmith Odeon in London, May 16, 1976, the band's fourth show of their first overseas trek.

01

ROCK AND ROLL ALL NITE

KISS FORM IN NEW YORK CITY

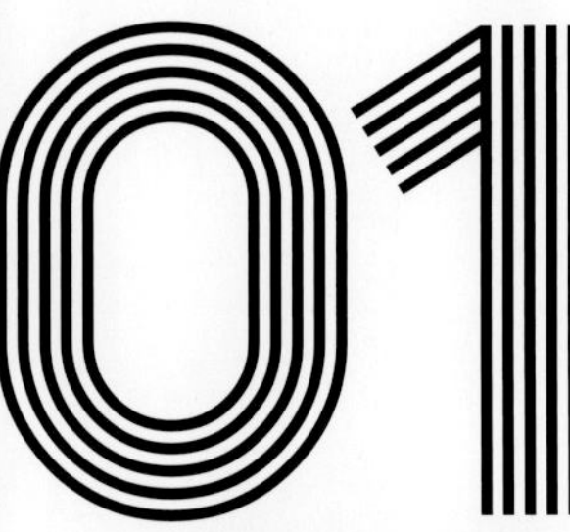

Wheeling and dealing in comic books.

This was Gene Simmons's most significant training before forming "the hottest band in the land." To be sure, apprenticing at *Vogue* magazine and teaching a classroom of sixth-graders helped as well, as did seeing The Beatles on *The Ed Sullivan Show*. But it was his inspiring origin story that built the backbone in the bassist necessary to push something like Kiss to the limit until it worked. Gene was born Chaim Witz, an only child, dirt-poor in Israel, with his family breaking down and Gene and his Holocaust survivor mother Flóra immigrating to New York, at which time Chaim becomes Gene Klein. Working his way through Jewish school, the public school system, and college, Gene soon was exercising his rock 'n' roll itch with bands like Lynx, Missing Links, Long Island Sounds, and Bullfrog Bheer, landing a record deal with Epic as founding member of Wicked Lester.

Formed in 1970 as Rainbow, Wicked Lester included in the band Gene's childhood friend and lead guitarist Stephen Coronel, who recommended that Stanley Eisen be brought in to play rhythm guitar. Moved from Manhattan to Queens with his parents and older sister, Stanley was also transformed by seeing The Beatles looming large on the small screen. His early training was on an acoustic guitar that he got when he was thirteen, with Stanley soon learning the folk-rock standards of the nascent hippie era and joining a band called Tree. In any event, Stanley had been Stephen's roommate and it was at their place that Gene first met him, with Stanley playing for Gene a song he had written called "Sunday Driver," soon to be "Let Me Know."

Moving forward, after Don Ellis at Epic rejected Wicked Lester's completed album, the band cleaved down the middle, with Gene and Stanley—now using the names Gene Simmons and Paul Stanley—hanging on to the Wicked Lester name and imagining a harder rocking direction for the band.

Enter Peter Criss, who had placed an ad in the back of *Rolling Stone* reading, "EXPD. ROCK & roll drummer looking for orig. grp. doing soft & hard music. Peter, Brooklyn." Peter Criss was born George Peter John Criscuola in Brooklyn, the eldest of five children. Taking lessons from jazz great Gene Krupa, Peter played with a number of bands before appearing on Chelsea's self-titled debut, issued in late 1970. By the time he met the Wicked Lester guys, that band had morphed into Lips, first a trio and then a duo featuring Peter and future songwriting partner Stan Penridge. Peter's acceptance into Wicked Lester was clinched when the guys checked out his playing at a small Italian club, and suddenly there he was singing as well, in a voice Paul admiringly likened to that of Wilson Pickett. Plus, Peter showed up to his first meeting with the guys—at Electric Lady earlier that same day—dressed to the nines like "a white Jimi Hendrix." His fashion sense and brash confidence had Gene and Paul thinking that this guy was a natural rock star.

Then came the band's hotshot lead guitarist. Born Paul Daniel Frehley, Ace—his friends in high school thought he was "ace" with the girls—grew up in the Bronx as the youngest of three children in a musical family. Local stardom came early, with a series of bit bands that had Ace dropping out of high school to keep up, only to return later and earn his diploma. Driving a cab and doing other odd jobs (Ace had some early training in graphic arts, as did Paul and Peter), Ace answered an ad in the *Village Voice* that read, "LEAD GUITARIST WANTED with Flash and Ability. Album Out Shortly. No time wasters please." This was Wicked Lester, with Ace winning the gig despite showing up to the first of his two auditions with two different-colored sneakers, crumpling up and tossing the band's "application form," and then jumping the line of hopefuls, all of which put Paul and Gene off. He even walked right up to the guys while Bob Kulick was auditioning and yanked his chord out and plugged his own in—"Shock Me" indeed.

By January 17, 1973, Ace was in as a member of Wicked Lester, with the band changing their name to Kiss in time for their first concert, January 30, 1973, at the Popcorn Club to an audience of fewer than ten people, mostly friends and family. Already the band was experimenting with makeup and a flashy show to go with their heavier material, none of which had impressed Epic A&R man Don Ellis, who had by this point rejected the band for a second time (granted, back in November of 1972, just before Ace had joined).

As for the name Kiss, Paul, Gene, and Peter had been driving around New York City when Peter had remarked that he had been in a band called Lips, with Paul then suggesting Kiss. Then, late January, Ace wrote the new name over a Wicked Lester poster rendering the "ss" in Kiss as stylized lightning bolts, with Paul then developing the lettering we see today, including the slightly asymmetrical presentation of the last two letters of the iconic all-caps logo.

The Popcorn Club debut—the venue's name was soon changed to the Coventry—was in fact a midweek three-night stand, for which the band was paid $50 a night. Although the makeup was worn, it wasn't until the March 9th and 10th shows at The Daisy ("Long Island's Only Heavy Rock Club") that the band's character-driven presentation was unleashed upon the world. As for the music, by this point the band had shed a few more Wicked Lester songs, presenting instead soon-to-be iconic songs like "Nothin' to Lose," "Let Me Know," "Watchin' You," "100,000 Years," "Deuce," "Strutter," and "Black Diamond." Also having been performed live by this point were "She," "Let Me Go, Rock 'n' Roll," and "Love Her All I Can." Unbeknownst, in composite, Kiss already had most of their first album sussed out as well as a head start on what would become *Hotter Than Hell* and *Dressed to Kill*. All they needed now was a record deal.

Gene feasts upon a pre-makeup press photo of Kiss in Munich, Germany, June 2, 1992.

02
SWEET PAIN

KISS SIGN WITH CASABLANCA RECORDS

Hot off their defining gigs at The Daisy, Kiss convened at Electric Lady Studios to record a five-song demo, engineered by Eddie Kramer, known by this point for his work with Johnny Winter, Humble Pie, Led Zeppelin, and, most substantially, Jimi Hendrix. The band had played a very loud private gig for Eddie at their rehearsal loft, running through fifteen songs, from which Eddie picked the highlights, namely "Deuce," "Strutter," "Black Diamond," "Cold Gin," and "Watchin' You," with the first four being destined for the band's debut album. Also at the showcase were Electric Lady engineer Ron Johnsen, who had recorded demos for Wicked Lester, and his wife Joyce, who apparently threw up in reaction to the volume. Eddie talks about the band not being particularly good, singling out Ace for being the proverbial card up the sleeve, the rock 'n' roll edge that just might make this band successful.

Armed with this demo, the band also worked out a new management deal, moving on from Lew Linet to film school graduate and cinematographer Bill Aucoin, who had been invited to the band's landmark July 13th showcase gig at the Hotel Diplomat, due to his work on a rock 'n' roll TV show called *Flipside*. Aucoin liked what he saw and, following another show a month later, was hired as the band's new manager on one condition: that he get them a record deal within two weeks. He indeed came through on the directive when on August 24 he secured a deal with Casablanca Records (actually called Emerald City at the beginning), a proposed venture to be run by Neil Bogart, formerly of Buddah Records, and, critically, soon to be funded by Warner Bros.—that is, until Neil had a falling-out with Warner over the label's attempts to bury the record after Kiss refused to ditch the makeup. The contract was officially inked on November 1, 1973, at which time the band was already putting the final touches on their first album.

Humphrey Bogart and the film *Casablanca* were the inspiration for the eventual name of Bogart's new imprint, along with the distinctive desert scene he'd use for his record labels, soon to add a splash of Hollywood to this most cinematic of bands. In fact, the launch party for Bogart's new venture was decorated as a tribute to the classic 1942 film. The festivities took place on February 18, 1974, in the Los Angeles Room at the Century Plaza Hotel in LA, with Kiss, the label's first signing, simultaneously celebrating the launch of Casablanca as well as the release of the band's first album. The party was themed as "A Night in Morocco." Along with prop camels and signature Rick's Café 1940s fashion (Neil wore a white tuxedo), Kiss played a twenty-minute set, complete with smoke, pyro, and a levitating drum riser. Guests included Alice Cooper, Iggy Pop, Michael Des Barres, Dick Clark, and journalists Lisa Robinson and Alison Steele. The LA rock glitterati were given $1,000 of fake money to gamble with at the faux gaming tables, with the ultimate prize being the Maltese falcon sculpture from the movie. After seeing the band, Alice Cooper quipped, "They're good, but they need a gimmick."

Indeed, the showcase in LA was a bit of a milestone for Kiss. All of the band's performances in 1973 had been in and around New York. Their first tour date proper had been just two weeks before LA, in Edmonton, Alberta, of all places, with two more Canadian dates taking place before the band played Long Beach Civic Auditorium the night before the label's launch party. There'd be one more LA show before the band would settle into a lifetime of touring beginning March 22, 1974.

Casablanca would go on to fly hard and high by the seat of its pants, cocaine and money everywhere, easy come, easy go. Kiss would spearhead the label's success, but also selling well (while being manipulated high up the Billboard charts) were Parliament, Donna Summer, and Village People. Hard rock and disco talk reverberating down the hallways was soon drowned out by fervent movie chatter, when a 1976 merger with Filmworks, generated hits with *The Deep* and *Midnight Express*.

Eventually, it would crash down like a house of cards, with accusations of mismanagement, financial improprieties, and rampant drug abuse tearing apart allegiances. Polygram acquired a 50 percent stake in 1977 and then the rest of it three years later, subsuming the once proud and feisty imprint as it carried on mostly with disco. In 1982, founder Neil Bogart died of cancer at the age of thirty-nine, with Kiss dedicating its *Creatures of the Night* album to the label's mercurial founder. Casablanca was relaunched in 2000 and again as an electronic imprint in 2012, but nothing could ever match the mania around the Casablanca offices in 1978 when Kiss and Donna Summer and "Macho Man" and "Y.M.C.A." were all the rage and all at once.

Below and opposite: Centennial Concert Hall, Winnipeg, Manitoba, May 16, 1974.

03

KISSIN' TIME
THE SELF-TITLED DEBUT

Dues paid: a few, not many. Prep work: actually, quite a lot.

Fact is, as the guys in Kiss approached their first album, they had a solid grounding in the rock 'n' roll business but were still, in the main, not what you would call seasoned veterans. There'd been the bit bands, but also an officially issued record from Peter and demo sessions and essentially a shelved record from Paul and Gene. Plus, they'd been playing live for what amounts to basically six months—again, a clutch of shows, but these were no road warriors.

Now all but signed up with Casablanca, the guys began work at Bell Studios mid-October 1973 with Kenny Kerner and Richie Wise, a couple of producers who had defected from Buddah along with Neil. Richie had also made two records as vocalist and guitarist for Kama Sutra/Buddah act Dust, with Kenny producing and contributing to essentially all the songwriting. Working long days, five days a week, the team was done by the time of the official signing, with Wise estimating that the sessions took thirteen days.

Kiss was issued on February 18, 1974, flipping out those flipping-through-the-record bins, but not exactly sending them across the orange shag carpet to the cashier, wallet flipped open and a fiver removed.

Backstage at the Long Beach Auditorium, May 31, 1974. *Rock Scene* **documented the rock 'n' roll party scene, primarily in New York City.**

Still, the album would make waves, becoming fervently discussed across the rock critic class and shortly thereafter by young teen boys across America. The topicality was twofold. First, there was the shocking Kabuki makeup of the band posed Beatles-like on the front cover—sensibly, this is the most refined the guys had ever looked to date, although the design on Peter, applied professionally this one time, would soon be simplified. Ace had surprised the guys by spray-painting his hair silver. Although they expressed reservations about how hard it was going to be to get the paint out, they applauded his commitment.

Beyond the confrontational confection of the cover, the music enclosed was uncommonly stomping and aggressive, especially for an American rock 'n' roll band. To be sure, the UK already had Black Sabbath, Deep Purple, and Uriah Heep, but as far as the States were concerned, it kinda went from Blue Cheer to The Stooges, MC5, Mountain, Cactus, Blue Öyster Cult, and then three concurrent acts in The New York Dolls, Aerosmith, and Montrose—the last being the smallest and the grandest at the same time as of 1973. Slim pickings, as they say. Excepting Montrose (who were about to fade fast), it could be argued that Kiss had just delivered the very first U.S. second-wave heavy rock album, soon to be joined by better Aerosmith records as well as Ted Nugent as a solo act, better BOC albums, and a few decent baby bands, the biggest being Boston. Rush also came onto the scene in 1974, and while we're talking about Canadians, the sum total of *Kiss* sounded like a heavy Bachman–Turner Overdrive album.

The album was composed mainly of songs already tried and tested onstage, navigable through smoke, fire, explosions, and flashing lights. Many formed the core of the Wicked Lest catalog. *Kiss* opens strong with "Strutter," a modern enough hard rocker using vestiges of the waning British blues boom (the boogie bit) against blustery, blue-collar riffing. This was written about a year before Ace joined the band and bears a rare Stanley/Simmons credit.

Even more sort of dated and rock 'n' rollsy is "Nothin' to Lose," which features fully Paul, Gene, and Peter singing, the latter being the hook and highlight of the track. This was the album's (and band's) first single, backed weirdly with the instrumental selection "Love Theme from Kiss," previously known as "Acrobat." Paul wrote concert staple "Firehouse," inspired by The Move's "Fire Brigade." Live, during this somewhat loping, funky hard rocker, Paul wears a fireman's hat and Gene, at the clanging conclusion of the song, breathes fire.

"Cold Gin," written by Ace, supports the idea that Kiss are one of the acts exploring this new heavy metal zone, where everybody in the band crowds around, warming their hands on a fiery riff burning in an oil drum. Closing the first side of the original vinyl is "Let Me Know," which began life as "Sunday Driver" and was later recorded by Wicked Lester. Old-school boogie pervades this one too, but the rest of it is melodic pop with a touch of glam, rather than the post-blues power chord riffing heard elsewhere.

Side two opens with a cover of "Kissin' Time," which was left off the first issue of the album but then quickly added as the label searched for a novelty hit. Despite it being a hit for Bobby Rydell in 1959, it's neither old rock 'n' roll nor, here, particularly pop, with Kiss slamming it with huge chords until it fits perfectly and poundingly with the rest of the record.

Gene framed Kiss classic "Deuce" on "Bitch" by The Rolling Stones, writing it on bass, hence its rhythmic aggression. It's the meanest heavy metal track on the album, sort of tied with "100,000 Years," which comes soon enough, after a spacey respite for the aforementioned "Love Theme from Kiss." Side two closes with the longest and most ambitious song on the album, even if "100,000 Years" evokes an air of prog rock. "Black Diamond" begins dramatically with Paul singing over acoustic guitar. Then we're into a tough rocker featuring a surprise lead vocalist—Peter Criss—who impresses with his phrasing, his soul, and the roughness of his natural voice.

Add it up, and *Kiss* is a strutting debut record with nothin' to lose, to be sure, somewhat brash and even stodgy at times. And yet at the core, it's a selection of tight, well-written songs, proven as such perhaps by how perennial so many of them would become in Kiss set lists over the decades that the band has been with us. Reaching #87 on the Billboard charts and selling seventy-five thousand copies during its relevant life cycle, *Kiss* fought its way to an RIAA gold certification on June 8, 1977, with the album also reaching gold in Canada—fateful indeed, given that the band kicked off its first tour ever in Edmonton, Alberta.

04

SEE YOU IN YOUR DREAMS

APPEARANCE ON ABC'S IN CONCERT

"America's Oldest Teenager," Dick Clark.

The day after the Casablanca launch party, Kiss found themselves at the Aquarius Theater in LA recording three songs live to be aired on ABC's *In Concert*, which was at this point a Dick Clark production and part of the network's Wide World of Entertainment portfolio.

When the show aired on March 29, it represented Kiss's first appearance on national television. Endearingly, Paul says he barely remembers the band's performance, given how starstruck he was at meeting Dick Clark, whom he had watched religiously, educating young Stanley Eisen on bands throughout the '60s. Paul assures us that Clark was considerate, calming, and polite when he visited them in their small and cluttered dressing room getting keyed up for the show. Gene remembers the magic moment much the same, with both of them issuing kind statements about Clark when he passed away in 2012 at the age of eighty-two.

With a turn of a revolving stage, Kiss followed Redbone, playing under a huge, lit rainbow, with the sizable Kiss light bulb logo tucked in beneath it. Paul struts up to the mic and says, "Hey world, we are Kiss! We want everybody here to come along with us. You've got nothin' to lose!" Into the band's song about (ostensibly) anal sex we go, with the guys sounding tight as a drum, heavy and rockin', selling the surprisingly numerous parts to their first single. Everybody sings, Peter drums like a punk rocker, and a party is in progress, with the band closing shop on the song with a deft unison lunge.

"Firehouse" follows, featuring Ace's rhythmic and musical solo and a detectable build of drama. There are smoke, sirens, red lights, and clanging bells, culminating in Gene's fire-breathing act. As a point of process (because it definitely was one), the band is now fully ensconced in black and silver and looking like a gang that shops at the same S&M shop—the Oakland Raiders on acid, we used to say as kids. Only Peter's makeup is a bit casual, and Paul's even brought a Flying V.

Then we're into a quickened "Black Diamond," with Peter screaming his way through the song with authority, occasionally conjuring Paul Rodgers with his pacing but mostly just vamping like a madman. Then we're into the kerranging power chord windup of the song, which takes a full minute as Peter's riser rises and the lights dim, giving way to eerie billowing blue smoke—the end.

As proud a moment as meeting Dick Clark was to arrive when the guys hustled their way back to their motel room after a concert at the Sunshine Inn in Asbury Park, New Jersey, to witness the airing of the show in late March. Paul recalls watching it on a "crappy TV," but rest assured, the band delivered, aided by the fact that *In Concert* was recorded particularly well compared with much of its competition. To be sure, Kiss looked and sounded powerful, making their first national spotlight a milestone of a stand.

Century Plaza Hotel, Los Angeles, February 18, 1974. This date was five shows into the band's first ever tour.

RECORDING KISS

A record so good they hadda name it twice? Kiss–*Kiss* is no Van Halen–Van *Halen*, but it's a more than sturdy effort, hatching many a Kiss classic for the ages. Part of the credit surely must go to the producers of the album, Kenny Kerner and Richie Wise, no more storied than the guys in the band, but just as intent on putting in a good day's work. As Richie relates, that's pretty much the theme all around.

"After the second Dust album, the one called *Hard Attack*, the label perceived that as a well-produced record," explains Wise. "I have in the back of my brain that I played it for some of the people at the label without telling them who it was, and none of them knew it was the guys they had released a previous album for, Dust (laughs). And Neil Bogart was part of that, and thought it was especially well produced. Before Neil signed Kiss to Casablanca, he'd given us the opportunity to go in with a couple of his acts on Kama Sutra/Buddah and produce them. And I was, at that point, breaking away from the rock 'n' roll lifestyle that Marc Bell, who became Marky Ramone, and Kenny Aaronson, who still to this day plays with everybody, were still part of. I got married and Dust sort of dissolved. Kenny Kerner, my partner, and the guy who was our original manager, and still to this day a friend, and somebody who knows more about the band than anybody, we decided to partner up and start producing. And Neil gave us the opportunity to do that when he signed Kiss to Casablanca. That led to a couple of albums with them."

Asked how he and Kenny split the duties, Richie says, "As a producer, I was the music guy. I was the player, the singer, the melodic guy, and so I got very involved with recording the arrangements with the band, producing, if you will, and directing how guitars and solos would be—going off on the music side. Kenny was very much more of a feel guy, and also more of the business side of the partnership.

"Paul never cared about playing anything other than rhythm," continues Richie, on the subject of roles in the band. "Paul was a great, great rhythm player. And I remember him even saying, 'I want to be the best rhythm player.' He was really into playing super-solid, super-in-time, super-effective rhythm guitar. Ace was Ace. He played basically the same stuff that I was playing in Dust and he played it well, had a good tone, knew how to use a Les Paul to his advantage. Ace was very, very easy to work with. Very consistent. But Paul, Paul especially was very focused on playing super-solid rhythm guitar. And I think that's very important—it was the foundation of Kiss."

Moving to the man at the back, "Peter Criss was a solid drummer; not very flashy, but I would say that he was perfect for the band. I'd just come from working with Marc, who was incredibly flashy, and Peter wasn't that kind of drummer. He laid down a really solid beat for them. Gene was actually a really good bass player, very tasty, played a lot of interesting bass parts that were not sort of basic. He would play more like a guitar player, playing the bass, finger-picking, but also with a pick—really solid."

While Richie fully appreciated the power of the first Montrose album and loves his Led Zeppelin, he didn't see any of that in Kiss. Nor much New York Dolls. He knew there was this new band out of Boston called Aerosmith making waves as well. "I never got a Led Zeppelin vibe from Kiss, or a blues rock vibe," reflects Richie. "That started with The Yardbirds. Obviously, the British rock influenced them. They don't sound anything like The Who, but I think they liked The Who. I remember Paul Stanley saying he liked Pete Townshend.

"But they were four really super guys," continues Wise, recalling the sessions. "Never had a word with them. They were really into it. They were the most focused band I had ever worked with. And I could say after producing records for thirty years, they would be the most focused band that I ever knew. From the very beginning, they knew what they wanted to do, who they wanted to be. Unlike Dust, where it was all completely organic, they put thought into it. Gene and Paul were certainly, certainly focused on becoming the biggest band in the world. That's what they wanted to do. And they would draw pictures of the boots they were going to design, and the clothes they were going to design. They really had it planned, what the makeup was going to look like. I mean, they were so in tune with what they thought, and it was all designed to get them successful. There was just no denying it. That is probably true of most bands that become that successful—they really know what they are, who they are, and what they're not."

But the fond memories end there. "I'd rather not talk about that," answers Richie, asked about the second record, *Hotter Than Hell*. "That album is a mistake, okay? That became a really screwed-up album. I love the first record. We had a good engineer on that album. The engineer that did that album was the guy that ended up doing the first Boston album and did a lot of other things too. The first album was real strong, real natural sounding. Bell Sound, in New York, built a better room that had a new console. I think it was one of the first ATI consoles, and me doing that for thirty years, I've worked with a lot of consoles. But the second album . . . I really don't like to even think about it. It's hard for me to listen to. I don't know why it wound up the way it did. Then again, some of my favorite albums sound like crap."

Gene sells the band to an industry showcase on the left coast, Century Plaza Hotel, Los Angeles, February 18, 1974.

WHILE RICHIE [WISE] FULLY APPRECIATED THE POWER OF THE FIRST MONTROSE ALBUM AND LOVES HIS LED ZEPPELIN, HE DIDN'T SEE ANY OF THAT IN KISS. NOR MUCH NEW YORK DOLLS. "OBVIOUSLY, THE BRITISH ROCK INFLUENCED THEM" . . . I REMEMBER PAUL STANLEY SAYING HE LIKED PETE TOWNSHEND.

05

C'MON AND LOVE ME

GENE INTERVIEWED ON
THE MIKE DOUGLAS SHOW

Talk show legend, Mike Douglas, 1979.

Making it national TV in stereo, Kiss showed up on *The Mike Douglas Show* on March 29, 1974, the same day that their ABC *In Concert* stand aired. But this was a little spicier, all 'round more revealing of what Kiss were about in the early stages. The trip to see the amiable talk show host was supposed to entail only a musical performance, but at the last minute, the band was asked if anybody wanted to be interviewed, with Gene stepping up.

Mike holds up a copy of *Kiss* and introduces Gene, who appears quite shocking and evil-looking, impossibly skinny in his high boots, slumped over like a ne'er-do-well punk. He flicks his tongue and hisses but doesn't say much, greeting the guests uncomfortably. Douglas calls for a close shot of the shoes, and then we get the classic exchange. Comedian Totie Fields opens with, "Incidentally, he's up for adoption," followed by some amusing eyerolls and "Is your mother watching today?" as Gene attempts to compare his own bat wings with Totie's festive blouse. Then it's "Wouldn't it be funny if under this he was just a nice Jewish boy?" Gene answers with, "You should only know," to which Fields replies, "I do. You can't hide the hook." At that point Gene's got nothing. He wrinkles his nose a few times, and Mike changes the subject, talking about the Kiss-sponsored kissing contest.

The winning couple of the event comes out, and there's a discussion about the prize trip to see a Kiss gig in Toronto being canceled. Gene explains that instead the couple will be flown to California and put on an eight-day cruise to Acapulco. He also says that they would advance to the world championship, and that Kiss are trying to get Howard Cosell to do the play-by-play. The interaction proceeds as it began, oscillating between both sides of cringe-worthy, but all told, Gene most definitely makes an impression, as self-professed "evil incarnate," as comic book character, as surly punk, and as rock star in the making. Also in there as well, it feels like Gene's gears are spinning as he tries to work out whether to drop the guise and emulate Alice Cooper's articulate and sociable talk show manner. Bottom line, with the flummoxed complexity and with Totie's barbs, it made for good TV.

After a "We'll be smack in a minute" message and commercial, all of Kiss appear, performing live—and not lip-synched—"Firehouse," slinky, funky, in the pocket, with Peter playing uncommonly busy. At the close, there's the signature smoke, sirens, and red flashing lights. Ace, having just knocked off the song's chunky axe solo, abusing his volume knob, after which Gene breathes fire (without incident) and plants his torch.

Unfortunately, Totie Fields, forty-four at the time, would die four years later due to complications from various ailments, including diabetes. Apparently, due to their revealing exchange, she and Gene had struck up and kept a friendship, right up to the time of her death.

A shot from the February 18, 1974, Century Plaza Hotel showcase gig in L.A. finds Gene inventing black metal.

06

TWO TIMER
HOTTER THAN HELL, THE SECOND ALBUM

"*Hotter Than Hell* was an interesting time because you have your whole life to write your first album and a few months to write your second," says Paul. "And that's an overwhelming task, intimidating too, because you don't have the safety or security of having had time to really pick and choose. So *Hotter Than Hell* was an interesting time, because we had to define who we were, after the first album, who we were going for from there. I like the album. I'm not fond of the way it sounds, overall. But I enjoyed making it, because it was our first time, literally living in a Ramada Inn in Los Angeles, and having a pretty wild lifestyle at that point. Certainly, what a lot of bands aspire to top or copy. You can tell all the stories you want—ours were true. We had a great time. It was our first brush with fame and all the trappings."

Hotter Than Hell in fact represents one of those instances where the oft-heard bromide about second albums rings true. The second Kiss album was issued hot on the heels of the first one, within the same year, on October 22, 1974. Once again, Richie Wise and Kenny Kerner were producing, but because the two had relocated to Los Angeles, that's where the album was recorded. Unfamiliarity with the recording studio, West LA's The Village or Village Recorders, resulted in a recording that was subpar. Specifically, the end product lacks in treble and is boomy and weirdly "gutted" at the drum end, especially with respect to the snare drum, which sounds small and noisy. Fans have debated the sound ever since and most have gotten used to it, comfortable with its "eccentricity." Bottom line: It hasn't stopped many Kiss scholars from calling *Hotter Than Hell* the best Kiss album of all time. As we see, Paul now recalls the experience fondly, but at the time he was not happy, having had a guitar stolen the very day they arrived in LA.

One happy place is the cover art. The back cover pictures, shot by Norman Seeff, arose from a drunken bacchanal of a photo shoot that made the band look even more alien and exotic than they did on the debut, like true rock stars, evil and even demonic. Then there's the added suggestion through the manga-styled graphics that the band had already been to Japan and back and lived to tell the tale.

Once inside the record (and acclimatized to the mix), the prepubescent purchaser of the product found himself confronted with a heavier and darker (or at least more "serious") version of the band versus that of the glammy debut. Fitting this narrative most accurately would be the lumbering opener "Got to Choose," the technical and modern "Parasite," and on side two of the original vinyl, the aggressive and percussive "Watchin' You" (long since written and performed by the band) and doomy closer "Strange Ways."

"Parasite" and "Strange Ways" were both written by Ace Frehley, but he's not singing them, Ace at this point still lacking the confidence to jump in and provide any lead vocals. Gene sings "Parasite" and Peter very memorably howls his way through "Strange Ways," although the latter is widely celebrated for featuring the top-rated Ace guitar solo of all time. "'Strange Ways' was a special solo," says Frehley. "I usually cut guitar solos in the control room, listening to the same monitors as the producer that I'm working with and the engineers I'm working with. But for that particular solo, I basically walked out in front of the Marshall stack and turned it to ten and just let it go. I think that solo was like one take."

Most depressive is the ballad "Goin' Blind," a curious cowrite between Gene and Steve Coronel that charts the relationship between a ninety-three-year-old man and his sixteen-year-old girlfriend! Elsewhere the album brightens. "Mainline," "Let Me Go, Rock 'n' Roll," and "Comin' Home" represent the band's regular pasting of pop to traditional boogie structures, while "All the Way" and "Hotter Than Hell" stack the power chords a mile high.

Hotter Than Hell was worthy enough—and promoted enough through live performance—to get certified gold appreciably quickly, achieving that status on June 23, 1977, even if it's never reached platinum. Still, its slow sales upon issue, hampered by the expiration of Casablanca's distribution deal with Warner Bros., caused Bogart to haul the band off the road and put them back in the studio a mere four months after the album hit the shops. The rushed follow-up wouldn't fare much better.

**Georgia Tech's Alexander
Memorial Coliseum,
Atlanta, Georgia,
December 1, 1974.**

Creem photographer
Robert Alford captured
the band at Michigan
Palace in Detroit on
December 20, 1974.

07

A MILLION TO ONE

TWO FANS FORM THE KISS ARMY

Your intrepid author has joined only four fan clubs in his time, and all of them as a teenager. Those would be the Saxon Militia, Motörheadbangers, whatever the Buffalo Sabres had going during the years of the French Connection, and finally, first of the brat pack, the Kiss Army, straight off the order form inside *Destroyer* back in 1976.

By that point the movement had evolved past its humble origins as the domain of a couple of Terre Haute, Indiana, Kiss fans, namely Bill Starkey and Jay Evans, who called local radio station WVTS threatening to burn the place down (this kind of talk was allowed in 1975) if Kiss wasn't played immediately. Starkey first heard of Kiss through the local newspaper, then saw them that night on *In Concert*. Fueling his enthusiasm for music, his dad worked as an expediter in the local Columbia record plant, one of three in the country that made all the records. Starkey Sr. would bring free records home and shortly thereafter brought home a copy of *Kiss*. What's more, Pops encouraged his kids and was getting a kick out of the brouhaha around this group Kiss. Next stop was December 8, 1974, in Evansville, Indiana, with Dad taking Starkey and his younger brother to see the band live for the first time. Then it was Mom's turn to take the kids to see them, in Indianapolis, three weeks later, with the guys going on after ZZ Top at an ungodly 12:30 a.m. Starkey couldn't wait to

report back to his buddy Jay Evans about the show, and this is where the hassling of the local FM station begins, with Evans coming up with the idea to identify themselves as the Kiss Army, allowing Starkey to be president and taking the title field marshall for himself.

Next it was back to the Convention Center in Indianapolis, April 22, 1975, this time with Kiss headlining over some Canadian band called Rush (note the theme here of hard rock bands hammering hard the Midwest, the part of the country that gave Aerosmith their "Blue Army"). Coming back down to earth, Starkey and Evans worked their way through the summer of 1975 at becoming thorns in the side at what were now two radio stations in town being harangued to play Kiss. They were taking their own albums into the stations if they were needed, they were making Kiss T-shirts, and people about town were now wearing the makeup and painting their cars with Kiss designs. All the while the radio stations kept getting calls from people about how they could join the Kiss Army.

Terre Haute then got a brand-new arena called the Hulman Centre, and Kiss were scheduled to play on November 21, 1975, flying high on the *Alive!* album released two months earlier. Starkey's promotional efforts on radio (Evans was in college by this point and

relinquishing duties) had helped make the ten-thousand-capacity show a sell-out, and Kiss wanted to meet the evangelist responsible. The town had pulled out all the stops for the arrival of the band. There were 200 fans at the airport as well as a jazz band, and the actual army was called to provide a Jeep escort down the main drag en route to the radio station on the outskirts of town. Later on, after interviews and Paul and Gene playing DJ, Starkey got to watch the show with Bill Aucoin from the side of the stage. During the third encore, Paul called him up onstage to present him with a plaque—earlier in the day, the mayor had given the band the key to the city.

Unbeknownst to Starkey, this would turn out to be the peak of his Kiss Army participation. Although early plans called for Starkey to run a full-on national Kiss Army from Terra Haute, Allan Miller from the New York office soon had to relay the news that the Kiss organization would have to take over, and that it was going to be run out of Los Angeles. The band's art director, Dennis Woloch, soon came up with the distinctive red, black, and orange Kiss Army logo and, as alluded to, the first call-to-arms took place inside the *Destroyer* album, with enlistment happening swiftly at the price of $5 per year. It was reported that at one point, the operation was being funded to the tune of $5,000 a day, en route to a peak membership of one hundred thousand fans.

Dedicated young fans at the Cow Palace in San Francisco. This was also the night Elvis Presley died, with Kiss playing "Jailhouse Rock" in his honor.

GREAT EXPECTATIONS

DRESSED TO KILL, THE THIRD ALBUM

After the bad vibes of California, Kiss wanted to record at home. So in February of 1975 they entered Electric Lady Studios to put down tracks for their third album. "Casablanca was in really bad shape financially," explains manager Bill Aucoin, "and Neil said me, 'Look, we can't afford to hire a producer; I'll produce the third album.' So *Dressed to Kill* was produced by Neil and the guys basically; all of them threw their hat into the ring because there wasn't any money to hire anybody." In the end, the band was credited along with Bogart, who Peter says was smoking too much pot and not hearing things correctly. For his part, Gene figures the end result sounds good, but that the songs were better across the first two records. Roiling beneath the surface was the fact that Bogart was trying to wrench management of the band away from Aucoin at the same time that he was romancing Aucoin's partner and comanager of Kiss, Joyce Biawitz, soon to be Joyce Bogart.

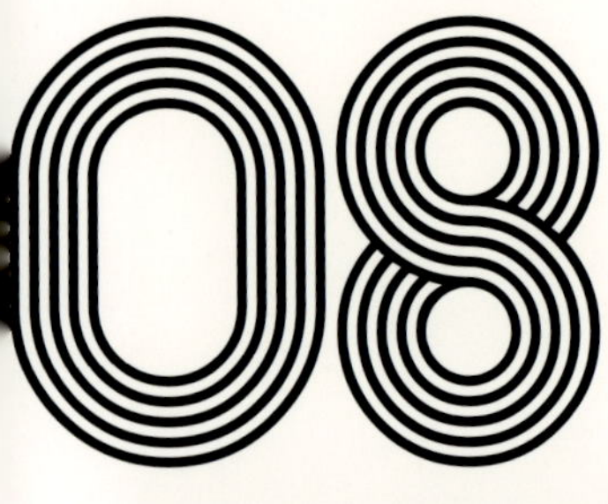

Affirms Larry Harris from the Casablanca perspective, "There was no money for costumes; again, at the beginning in the label's history, we were having financial problems. So it wound up some of the guys from Kiss wore Neil Bogart's suits for that cover (laughs). But the album was fine. We never thought any of them weren't. Well, that's not true. The solo albums we didn't like—any of them. But we had to do them because of contract rules and stuff. We didn't think any of their albums were bad. I mean, we were always into them. Maybe we talked ourselves into being excited, but we were always excited with their new albums."

Truth be told, everybody's got a different story on whose suits were used for the iconic Bob Gruen cover shoot, which took place on the southwest corner of 8th Avenue and 23rd street, facing north. Consensus is that Peter owned suits, so he's wearing one of his own, but Gruen says Gene is wearing one of his, along with his wife's clogs. Gene says Aucoin contributed the suit he's wearing, tan while everyone else's is dark. It's definitely way too small, as is Paul's, whereas Ace and Peter look comfortable. One extravagance allowed with respect to the cover art was the blind embossing for the Kiss logos ringing the street shot.

There were three clear winners on *Dressed to Kill,* underscored when "C'mon and Love Me," "Rock Bottom," and "Rock and Roll All Nite" made the subsequent live album, and surprisingly no others from the studio album being promoted on the tour. "Rock and Roll All Nite"/"Getaway" was issued as the first single two weeks after the album's March 19, 1975, release date but died a death after reaching #69 on the Billboard charts. The version from the live album would fare much better, but it's the studio take that would become a classic rock staple moving forward, a sort of latent hit for the band similar to what happened to Aerosmith with "Dream On."

"I remember recording 'Rock and Roll All Nite,'" says Ace, "and Neil Bogart and a whole bunch of people in the studio basically came in from the control room and everybody just started singing the chorus toward the end. It was a lot of fun, kind of a special night. That also had 'She,' which is a great song—I love it. Gene cowrote that with Steve Coronel, who was the guitarist in the original lineup prior to Kiss when they called themselves Wicked Lester." Despite its modern energy and sturdy riff, "Love Her All I Can" also came from the old days, while, ill advisedly, the most dated-sounding song on the album, "Room Service," was chosen to open the record.

"C'mon and Love Me," also backed with "Getaway," was issued as the second and last single but did not chart. The album at large got to an impressive #32 on the Billboard grid and to #37 at Cashbox, but attendant sales did not follow. Still, the album was certified gold in 1977, testimony to the general high quality of the material, despite Gene's misgivings.

Besides the three flagship tracks, lumbering hard rocker "She" eventually became a celebrated fan favorite, as did the quick-paced "Getaway," written by Ace but sung by Peter. As for the rest of *Dressed to Kill*, call it efficient, locked down, even businesslike, made buoyant through fastidious, perky production, an effect achieved through the use of acoustic guitar massaged in with the electrics as well as an excellent capturing of Peter's drums and cymbals, a noticeable improvement over what we heard on *Hotter Than Hell*.

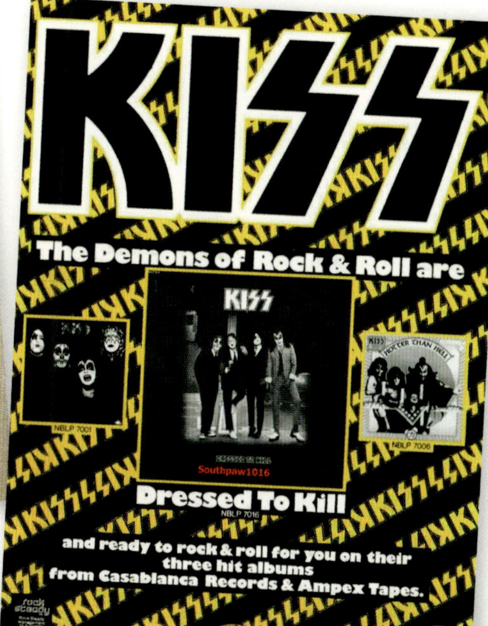

Los Angeles,
January 1975.

09

HOTTER THAN HELL

ALIVE!, A DOUBLE LIVE ALBUM

With Kiss suing Neil Bogart for nonpayment of royalties, and thus with no money coming in, it was up to Bill Aucoin to personally finance the *Dressed to Kill* tour, which led to the cheapest option available for a next record—something live.

Issued on September 10, 1975, *Alive!* was an explosive blast of sixteen hard and heavy Kiss songs. The iconic front cover captured the magic of the band's stage show perfectly, while the back jacket offered an iconic crowd shot taken by Fin Costello at Cobo Hall in Detroit. Inside the gatefold of the double album was a reminder that there are three other great Kiss albums still available. Then there was an LP-sized eight-page booklet featuring nineteen photos, each one every bit as transgressive and exciting as the cover shot.

Now, don't come here for the party line about the first three records "not capturing what the band sounded like live." *Kiss* and *Hotter Than Hell* sound visceral enough, leaving only *Dressed to Kill,* and even that one just does what a studio album's supposed to do. What *Alive!* does, however, is serve as a greatest-hits album with all of the songs subject to the same production values, Eddie Kramer creating a presentation that considers the best of all three sound pictures thus far while cranking the bass, improving the sound of Peter's toms, and sticking on crowd sound throughout, when most live albums faded the crowd out once the songs got going.

There are also the notorious overdubs (including crowd) in all departments, rhythm guitar, lead guitar, vocals, and even drums, which has been admitted by Peter on account of his gradual speeding up of the songs. But it's not everything, given the fact that Casablanca was in serious debt and the band was given only three weeks, working at Electric Lady, to fix things. Plus, they were a tight live act to boot and had four shows—Detroit; Cleveland; Davenport, Iowa; and Wildwood, New Jersey—with which to work. As Gene puts it, the guys jumped around so much that they'd regularly hit bum notes or not get back to the microphone in time after some burst of fire or choreographed move, even if they tried to tone down the antics for the capturing of these shows.

Highlights include the iconic "hottest band in the land" introduction and opening explosion for "Deuce" and then the album's two endings, more explosions at the end of side three with the dramatic closing section of "Black Diamond," but then more music and a windup of side four with an ebullient and jammy "Let Me Go, Rock 'n' Roll." Also entertaining are Paul's tongue-in-cheek stage raps, even if they drag somewhat on the twelve-minute version of "100,000 Years"—by that point we're already worn out, having sat through Peter's curiously juvenile drum solo.

Issued as a single was the *Alive!* version of "Rock and Roll All Nite" backed with the studio version, which, as discussed, took on a life of its own, becoming more of an enduring hit than the live take, which nonetheless got to #12 at the time. *Alive!* managed #9 on the Billboard charts and famously saved Casablanca and Kiss, certifying gold within a couple months of its release. It's famously one of these records due for a recount and recertification to at least platinum, given that an estimated nine million copies have been sold worldwide.

Cobo Hall, Detroit,
Michigan, May 16, 1975.
This was one of the
shows from which *Alive!*
was drawn.

Backstage at Cobo Hall in the band's stronghold of Detroit, May 16, 1975. The Fin Costello shot used on the *Alive!* album cover was taken at rehearsal sessions from the previous couple of days.

Cobo Hall, Detroit,
Michigan, May 16, 1975.
Ace hoists a bottle of
the notorious Mateus
rosé wine, popular in
the '70s.

10

BABY DRIVER

KISS TAKE OVER CADILLAC, MICHIGAN

If the live album was a publicity stunt of sorts, a month later, Kiss were back at it, traveling to Cadillac, Michigan (population ten thousand), to play a high school homecoming concert and more. The story is this: The Cadillac Vikings high school football team had enjoyed their 1973 season, trouncing the opposition going undefeated with nine wins. But they opened the 1974 season with two losses, and assistant coach Jim Neff was tasked with finding some suitable rock 'n' roll to play in the locker room (and for away games, on the bus) to pump the guys up. Having seen the band in Flint, he instantly picked Kiss (which also stood for the team's philosophy, "keep it simple, stupid") and the team won their next seven games en route to a conference cochampionship.

Kiss heard the story and decided to adopt the team, so to speak, checking in by phone calls and letters throughout the season. In the fall of 1975, Neff wondered if, given that Kiss were playing Kalamazoo (145 miles (233 km) away) just before Cadillac's homecoming, they could swing by and sign some autographs. Kiss said they'd do better than that; they'd bring the whole show.

The guys arrived on October 9, staying at the sixty-six-room Caberfae Motor Lodge. On that Thursday, the band played the Cadillac high school gym to a crowd of about two thousand, with the only concession being that Gene was asked not to spit blood (he didn't). The logo onstage was student-made because the one the band brought wouldn't fit. As for breathing fire, that was allowed and also put to second use for the lighting of the homecoming bonfire.

They mugged for pictures on the football field with the team and the cheerleaders and the firemen at the local fire station. They participated in a parade, sitting on top of a car and tossing out Hershey Kisses. Hundreds of residents, from toddlers up through school staff and city councilors, wore the makeup—in fact, for the breakfast meeting on the Friday after the concert, Kiss applied the makeup to the mayor and his staff themselves. After receiving the key to the city, Paul said, "On behalf of Kiss, after getting the key to the city, I hope you never change the locks."

When it was time for the band to leave, Kiss surprised the town by having a helicopter land in the middle of the football field to whisk the band away. As the helicopter rose into the air, the band tossed out flyers that said "CADILLAC HIGH—KISS LOVES YOU!" Due to the wind created by the helicopter, many of the four thousand flyers were blown outside of the football field area and into adjacent Cadillac. Then it was back to the reality of Kiss as a struggling rock 'n' roll band still paying for Casablanca's debacle with the Johnny Carson album: The helicopter pilot was told to land just over a hill and out of sight and earshot from the band's grand exit because that's all Aucoin and the guys could afford. Then they jumped into cars and headed to the airport.

Celebrating the forty-year anniversary of the event, Cadillac hosted the Kiss Cadillac Homecoming 40th Anniversary Celebration, highlighted by the dedication of a laser-etched memorial stone. Made of black granite and weighing in at 5,000 pounds (2.268 kg), it still reigns as the only Kiss "monument" in the world.

Kiss take to the field at Cadillac
High School in Cadillac, Michigan,
October 9, 1975.

11
STRUTTER
ALIVE! GOES GOLD

The *Alive!* album sold well instantly, achieving RIAA gold status on December 4, 1975, en route to spending 17 weeks on the Billboard charts and 110 weeks on the Cashbox chart, where, like Billboard, it achieved a #9 placement. *Circus* magazine's readers poll put the record as the second best of the year, after Led Zeppelin's *Physical Graffiti*. Bottom line, Kiss mania had begun, with the band reacting in kind, touring hard throughout October, November, and December, all shows in America, to close out the year.

In February 1975, Blue Öyster Cult, somewhat local mentors to Kiss, had issued a double live album after just three studio albums. *On Your Feet or On Your Knees* would represent an end-marker before a huge shift in sound for BÖC, and Kiss were inclined to muse in interviews about a similar situation for themselves, hoping that *Alive!* would serve as a celebration of the band's three records before they began a new chapter. Rush, who supported Kiss in the early days, would follow suit with *All the World's a Stage*, going double live after four albums. Kiss's success with *Alive!* would go on to inspire a golden era of commercially successful or at least welcome and well-regarded live albums for hard rock bands in the late '70s with the likes of Foghat, Thin Lizzy, UFO, Bachman–Turner Overdrive, Lynyrd Skynyrd, Ted Nugent, Aerosmith, Peter Frampton, The Pat Travers Band, and Kiss-label mates Angel (in 1980) all trying their hand at the game.

Whether all of them were inspired by Kiss is not important, although it would be hard not to notice the excitement *Alive!* generated in the industry. Fact is, the album is considered—when live albums are included in the mix—by most Kiss fans to be the pinnacle of the band's achievement on record. As well, I'd have to say that from the many interviews I've done with rock stars, Kiss is second only to The Beatles in causing future rock stars to happen, and when it does by way of Kiss, it's often most saliently by way of *Alive!*.

But yes, *Alive!* going gold indeed serves as a key highlight for the band, first because it happened so quickly, demonstrating cause and effect, but also because of the desperation back at the label for a hit. Fortunately at the same time, Casablanca was starting to see some success with both Parliament and Donna Summer, whose song "Love to Love You Baby" had become a major disco hit, catapulting the album of the same name toward gold status into January 1976. Parliament's *Mothership Connection* would go gold three months later and then platinum in September.

The always improving Kiss show, now directly financed by Bill Aucoin to the tune of $300,000, was paying dividends as well, working a feedback loop with the mania over the album. In September the band was playing ambitious venues but averaging crowds of about three thousand. The following month this was up to five and six thousand and then into November eight to eleven thousand (the band did two sold-out nights in Flint, Michigan, at fifty-three hundred each), en route to a draw of nearly twenty-two thousand for a sold-out Capital Centre show in Landover, Maryland, on November 30. December's numbers reflected a mix of the October and November results, but then again, Kiss had long committed themselves to playing every B, C, and D city across America and then hitting them all again months later. Many of these small blue-collar cities—and most definitely their smaller venues—would not be seeing Kiss again after the success of *Alive!*, not only in terms of its record sales but also due to its promotional effect on ticket sales.

The band receive their gold records for *Alive!* at the Nassau Coliseum, Long Island, New York, December 31, 1975.

12
HEAVEN'S ON FIRE
DESTROYER

Kiss chirped moderately about raising their game for the next studio album, or at least Paul and Gene did, not that they had any big ideas. In the end, it was enough that they were open to the possibilities, because when Alice Cooper and Lou Reed producer Bob Ezrin entered the picture, well, school was in, not for the summer but for a few days in September and then a couple weeks in January.

"I found myself in the stairwell with them at City Television in Toronto," says Ezrin. "I was going down as they were coming up the stairs, to be interviewed, and I stopped Paul Stanley on the stairs and said, 'Hi, I'm Bob Ezrin.' They knew who I was from the Alice Cooper stuff, I guess, and I said, 'Look, I hear you guys are amazing; if you're . . . are you happy with your records?' And Stanley looked at me like I was a Martian and said, 'What do you mean?' 'Well, you know, if at any point you decide you are not happy with the records you're making, call me; I would love to work with you.' And sure enough, I got the call."

Working at Electric Lady and the Record Plant, the band was put through the paces like they never had been before. Peter and Ace both revolted, not showing up on time or not at all, with Ezrin calling Dick Wagner in for the odd guitar part if and when needed. A recalcitrant Ace told me, "Working with Bob Ezrin was different. He was kind of a dictator. He had new ideas, and some of it didn't always go with the flow of the way everybody thought things should go. But in retrospect, Bob had a lot more knowledge than we did at the time, and we were wrong and he was right. Because that album stands the test of time. 'Detroit Rock City' is a real kick-ass song, a lot of fun. It's basically Kiss's tribute to the second city that kind of gave us life. Obviously, New York was the first. But a lot of people in the early days thought we were from Detroit because we kind of broke out of Detroit. Then there's 'God of Thunder,' which basically features Gene flying—that's just a good heavy metal anthem."

"Detroit Rock City," fronted with an extended sort of radio play, was the most ambitious heavy metal song the band had ever assembled, followed pretty closely by "King of the Night Time World" and "God of Thunder." Even "Shout It Out Loud," "Sweet Pain," and "Flaming Youth," more traditional Kiss, were ambitious in arrangement. But then there's Kim Fowley cowrite "Do You Love Me," with

Let it bleed. Gene works the lower end, Toledo, Ohio, July 30, 1976.

its haunting closing soundscape, and "Great Expectations," an orchestrated ballad with choir and grand piano augmentation.

Most egregious was the Peter Criss ballad "Beth," which had begun life as "Beck." Three singles had come and gone from the album, with "Beth" taking up space as the B side of the third, "Detroit Rock City." DJs started playing the shockingly easy listening and drumless song, and soon it became the fourth kick at the cat (so to speak), reaching #7 on the Billboard charts and certifying as a gold single, with *Destroyer* itself peaking at #11 in May 1976 and spending seventy-eight weeks on the charts.

"No one wanted it on the album," explains manager Bill Aucoin. "I had to kind of demand that it went on. For obvious reasons, they were saying, 'It wasn't a Kiss song; why did we do this anyway?' And part of the reason I got it on there was that Peter and Ace felt so bad about this whole album and not getting along with Bob that when I knew that 'Beth' was absolutely a hit song, I just said to Gene and Paul, 'Look, for Peter's sake and for the album's sake, we have to put this on. At

least it's a rock 'n' roll song in terms of what happens in the lyric to an artist, and we have to go with it.'"

"Bob Ezrin was a genius and an eccentric," continues Aucoin, "exactly the best of both worlds for me. It wasn't necessarily for the group in the sense that Ace and Peter just didn't get along with Bob at all; it was oil and water. On the other hand, Gene and Paul did, and Bob was strong enough to pull it all through. We could all get ideas to Bob, and he could get them done. He's just brilliant. I love the guy to this day—he is one of the best producers there is out there."

Destroyer was issued on March 15, 1976, fronted with a dramatic comic-style illustration featuring the members of the band as superheroes dancing upon (or floating over) the ruins of a burning city. Artist Ken Kelly had also done the *Rising* cover for Rainbow (issued two months later), and he'd soon be back for another fan favorite in *Love Gun*. Within

a month of its release, *Destroyer* had been certified gold, en route to platinum status in November. It's now widely ranked at the top of best-Kiss-albums lists, and the band loves it as well with fully five tracks from the record becoming perennial live favorites.

At the time? Not so much. Critics hated the album, finding it bloated and pretentious.

"They actually fired me after the record," laughs Ezrin, "like a couple of months later, just after it had come out and got some devastating reviews from the Kiss fanatical journalists like Dave Marsh and people like that, who basically cut it to shreds. The manager had called my lawyer and said how disappointed they were, and that I'd failed to capture the Kiss sound (laughs). And so I walked. The purist rock press had thought I had turned them into a Las Vegas act. They like the rawness and the mistakes and the changes in tempo and the bad lyrics and all that stuff. And that's fine—they can like that stuff. But

that doesn't resonate with the largest portion of the population. And clearly, this album did! It was—and remains—their best-selling record ever. It got everybody's attention and struck everyone's fancy, because it was theatrical, because it was bigger than life, because it had sound effects and strange things going on. It really captured people's imagination."

Gene checks the backseat accommodations of the *Munster Koach*, the iconic TV car created by famed custom car builder George Barris.

Kiss greet fans at Detroit Metro Airport after touchdown in January 1976.

13

CREATURES OF THE NIGHT

THE PAUL LYNDE HALLOWEEN SPECIAL

Comedian Paul Lynde was a huge TV personality in the '70s, his status established through his ten appearances on *Bewitched* from 1965 to 1971. But by the time *The Paul Lynde Halloween Special* aired on October 29, 1976, it was more for his epic run on *Hollywood Squares,* on which his comedic chops are legendary—and often themed upon his barely closeted homosexuality. Sadly, the world would lose Lynde only six years later at the age of fifty-five, when he died in his sleep from an apparent heart attack.

The '70s marked the golden age of the variety show specials, but this one was extra spicy, given the reappearance of Margaret Hamilton in her role as the Wicked Witch of the West from *The Wizard of Oz* after nearly forty years dead under the house. Variety circuit regular Tim Conway was also aboard for the fun, as were Betty White and Florence Henderson, with Donny and Marie Osmond appearing at the beginning and only once as surprise guests. Billie Hayes appeared as a second witch, reprising her role as Witchiepoo from *H.R. Pufnstuf.*

Then there was Kiss. Bill Aucoin had originally turned the opportunity down, but on second thought appreciated what the writers were trying to do with the one-hour show. As well, *Destroyer* was fading a little faster than the organization would have liked, having fallen off the charts at the end of August (then again, *Rock and Roll Over* was just around the corner). Plus, this would mark the band's first national TV appearance in prime time and, as Paul would say when asked if he was a ham, "Ham? I'm the whole pig."

Kiss show up for the first time at about the halfway mark when the Wicked Witch offers Lynde "a little chamber music." They descend from a cage in a puff of smoke and break into "Detroit Rock City." The mimed performance allows for maximum jumping around, but the guys do a great job of throwing shapes to the track, particularly Paul with the vocals.

Next, when the witches wish for a trip to a "Hollywood disco" (there's a three-wishes narrative to the show), Peter follows a Florence Henderson musical number with his mimed rendition of "Beth." He's at the piano, mood lighting provided by a candelabra, in a sort of sumptuous book-lined study setting. Paul, Ace, and Gene appear at the end, and then Lynde goes over to meet the band, saying, "Well, just what I've always wanted—four kisses on the first date." After a few

more amusing quips (with the band playing it straight, deadpanning), Lynde then asks for one more wish, that Kiss play another number. It's granted and the guys tear into "King of the Night Time World," lit by torches, candles, and then copious real pyro. Gene breathes fire and the cast sashays onto the dance floor for a closing disco number while Kiss look on disapprovingly from the balcony.

Quick-paced, heartwarming, and genuinely funny, *The Paul Lynde Halloween Special* was a success all around, with everybody talking about Kiss at school the next day to the clang of lockers. Given the large audience in prime time, the appearance marked a key step in mainstreaming the band that much further. If it worked for Alice Cooper, surely it could work for a band self-described as "four Alice Coopers."

14

ROCKIN' IN THE USA
ROCK AND ROLL OVER

It's up for conjecture: Had *Destroyer*'s effective life cycle been twelve or eighteen months instead of seven, would the band have seen steady or rising sales and made a second record with Bob Ezrin? We'll never know, because before the year was out, on November 11, 1976, the band was back with the Eddie Kramer–produced *Rock and Roll Over*, the fifth Kiss studio album in three years.

The brief was to get back to roots, put the making of "studio" albums aside, with the band literally not recording in a studio but rather the Star Theatre in Nanuet, just north of Manhattan. Kramer communicated with the band via video link from his control/recording room while the band recorded in the theater, on the venue's sunken stage, amps facing away, the goys occasionally moving around into various hallways for increased echo. Peter, on the other hand, was set up in a bathroom, which he loved, given how loud the drums sounded. He would prank the guys by disappearing or putting drawings up in front of the camera lens, irking Kramer, who wanted to get the record finished. Making the record in a theater with Kramer was good for band unity. Both Peter and Ace enjoyed the experience, and both of them liked Kramer. Plus, Ace had just married Jeanette and bought a new house, a mere fifteen minutes away from Nanuet.

As for the final results, *Rock and Roll Over*, compared with *Destroyer*, indeed sounded like a collection of simple Kiss songs, a logical next step from *Dressed to Kill*. At the heavy end there was the flash opener "I Want You," "Baby Driver" (sung by Peter), and the last song on side two, "Makin' Love." The rest is meat-and-potatoes Kiss, essentially poppy hard rock played straight and regularly laced with references to boogie rock like the old days, but with dirtier lyrics. The biggest outlier was "Hard Luck Woman," written by Paul and offered to Rod Stewart—it sounds like "Maggie May," although Paul says it's also influenced by Looking Glass hit "Brandy"—who declined to take the bait. Back in the Kiss camp, Paul was planning to sing it, but Gene suggested Peter instead. Now it sounded even more like a Rod Stewart song, plus it was clearly the second coming of "Beth," almost as much of a ballad, save for the fact that it's got drums.

"Hard Luck Woman" got to #15 on the Billboard charts, while the follow-up single "Calling Dr. Love" managed a #16 placement. The album itself got to #11 and represented the first time Kiss had an album that shipped gold. Within two months it was platinum, although no further certification has been met to date. For cover art, the band went with an illustration by graphic artist Michael Doret, who also created the logo for the New York Knicks. As with *Hotter Than Hell*, there's a Japanese flavor to the distinctive geometric design, one in which there is no correct top, bottom, left, or right orientation.

As for the sonic qualities Kramer and the guys got out of the Star Theatre, *Rock and Roll Over* doesn't sound as good as *Destroyer*, but it's also no disaster either, sounding like the mean/median/average of what the guys did on the first three albums. To be sure, it comes across as less dynamic—cheaper, frankly—than most albums of the day, but if the mandate was to "go back to the roots," well, *Rock and Roll Over* is mission accomplished in all departments.

Kiss fans (and Atlanta-based promoter Alex Cooley, far right) in their Kiss-inspired outfits pose with the band in a contest to help fight Muscular Dystrophy. The event took place at Peaches Records in Atlanta, Georgia, August 14, 1976.

Ace keeps his chops up backstage on the *Rock and Roll Over* tour in New York City, February 1977.

15

A WORLD WITHOUT HEROES

KISS AND MARVEL COMICS COLLABORATE

Kiss first appeared in comic book form in Marvel Comics' *Howard the Duck*, twice in issues #12 and #13, in May and June of 1977, respectively. But the big launch was about to come. Kiss were about to star in the Marvel Comics Super Special! series as the subject of issue #1. The series would soon become movie-themed, but Kiss would feature in the first one as well as #5 in 1978, with The Beatles featuring in #4.

For the media launch of the book on May 26, 1977, Kiss boarded a DC-3 prop plane and flew to Buffalo, New York. They then traveled by black limousine to Depew, just east of the city, accompanied by a Brinks armored truck. Inside the truck was a medical box. Inside the box were vials of blood from each of the four Kiss members, drawn by a nurse backstage at a concert stop on February 21 in Nassau, after which it was subject to guarded refrigeration.

At the Borden Chemical Plant in Depew, the guys poured their blood into a vat of red printer's ink, which was to be used on the comic book, the idea, of course, being that the Kiss comic book was going to be printed in the band's own blood. A notary public was on hand to make things official, stamping and signing a document, which the four Kiss members also signed. Also witnessing was band photographer Bob Gruen and Marvel legend Stan Lee, who had traveled with the band from New York on the chartered plane. Lee was an idol to Gene, who religiously read his work when growing up. As a kid, he even sent a postcard to Lee and got a reply back saying "Never give up." Both Gene and Lee had changed their names to sound less Jewish. When they met, Gene told him that the bat wings on his costume were inspired by a Lee character called Black Bolt.

The forty-page issue, printed in comparatively larger magazine format dimensions, premiered on June 20, 1977 (with a cover date of September 1977), to coincide with the release date of the band's sixth studio album, *Love Gun*. The story line pitted Kiss as superheroes called The Demon, The Starchild, The Cat, and The Space Ace in battle with Dr. Doom, along with other features on the band plus previously unseen photographs. The print run is said to have been nine hundred thousand with sales pretty quickly of half a million copies. This is apparently enough for the book to be the biggest-selling comic book of all time for the next thirteen years, when it was unseated by Todd McFarlane's *Spider-Man* as #1 in 1990.

Issue #5, released on August 15, 1978, clocked in at fifty-six pages and featured on its back cover an ad for the four simultaneously issued Kiss solo albums. It took place in "a country of the mind" called "The Land of Khyscz." Through the pair of big books, Gene had finally achieved his dream of becoming very much the pop culture standard of a superhero (he says that he's the only guy in the band who likes comic books), while Space Ace got to show off his galactic superpowers. As well, the series touched off a long association between Kiss and comic books to this day across myriad publishers, with *Kiss 4K— Legends Never Die: Destroyer Edition*, at 20" × 30" (50 x 76 cm) holding the distinction as one of the largest comics ever printed.

Comic book hero Gene Simmons with Denny Sanders from WEWS-TV at an in-store appearance in Cleveland, Ohio.

16

LOVE'S A DEADLY WEAPON

LOVE GUN

Album, tour, album, tour, strike while the iron's hot . . . it's a rock 'n' roll manager's dream, and Kiss were happy to oblige, while also executing their first tour of Japan and making comic books with their own blood on their days off. *Love Gun*, issued on June 30, 1977, is literally a hot iron, pushed into stores to the tune of a million copies presold and hence platinum on day one. To make the album, the band entered the familiar Record Plant studio in New York in May 1977, working once again with Eddie Kramer.

There's zero change to the formula used last time out, save for the debut of Ace Frehley taking a lead vocal for the first time. "Shock Me" is one of the heavier songs on the record and was inspired by an incident at a show in Florida in December the previous year where Ace touched an ungrounded railing and received a shock hefty enough to knock him to the ground and delay the show for half an hour. Ace played all the guitars and bass on the song, and for his vocal, he was so nervous that he sang the song while flat on his back so that he wouldn't have to see anybody while singing. As Ace told me, "I remember the first time I sang it live was at Madison Square Garden. Once I got that off my chest, I wanted to do more. That broke the ice for me as a lead vocalist because I joined a band with three lead vocalists—Paul, Gene, and Peter—and so I was a little intimidated initially. It took a while for me to get up enough nerve to sing a lead vocal for myself. We all have different voices. Peter's voice is grittier, as is Gene's. Paul has a great voice, and it's maybe more pop-orientated. I don't even consider myself a lead singer, but I think my voice has a lot of character because I grew up in the Bronx and I still haven't been able to shed my accent."

Also on the heavy side is opener "I Stole Your Love," with a riff that Paul admits was influenced by Deep Purple "Burn." The last of the three harder rockers is the title track, with its aggressive machine gun riff to announce the song—included inside the record jacket was your very own die-cut cardboard "love gun."

There's the requisite Peter vocal, only this time it's on a rocker called "Hooligan." Kramer really liked Peter's voice and wanted him to sing more songs on the album, which caused some friction with Paul, who was intent on guarding his territory. With no "Beth" or "Hard Luck Woman" in sight, the closest thing to a ballad is a cover of The Crystals' "Then He Kissed Me," rebranded as "Then She Kissed Me." The song exemplifies the '60s girl group influence one finds on New York rock bands like Kiss and Blue Öyster Cult and more pointedly The Dictators and The New York Dolls.

That's it for any degree of outlier. The rest of the album plays to the band's strengths as purveyors of a sort of puerile pop metal, the guys proving their fearlessness at writing and playing below their capabilities (and below the belt), happy to serve simple hard rock to teenagers. "Tomorrow and Tonight" was designed as a follow-up to "Rock and Roll All Nite," while "Plaster Caster" is a song in homage to Cynthia Albritton, a groupie who gained notoriety for casting in plaster the erect penises of rock stars, and "Almost Human" finds the band uncommonly percussive and funky with their pop metal.

An interesting story about "Christine Sixteen" and "Got Love for Sale" has Gene doing demo versions of the songs with Eddie and Alex Van Halen—Gene was working in a management capacity and trying to get Van Halen a record deal. On the demo for the former, Eddie does a rare double-tracked guitar solo that Gene liked so much, he had Ace play it the same way. The talented brothers also played on a demo version of "Tunnel of Love," which got reworked for Gene's solo album.

Back in 2005, Paul explained to me, "*Rock and Roll Over* and *Love Gun* are very similar. They followed each other very naturally. Sometimes we can make a conscious effort to regain something that was on a previous album, and if that album was too long ago, the chances are that it will be a noble attempt, but you're too far past it to actually go back to it. The fact that *Love Gun* and *Rock and Roll Over* followed each other, and were done at a certain point in our career where things were pretty much status quo from one to the other, makes for them to be similar and consistent."

For artwork, the band commissioned realist illustrator Ken Kelly, last on board for the iconic *Destroyer* sleeve. Now our heroes stood on a smoky stage flanked by marble columns in front of prostrated female sirens painted like Kiss and pining.

Launched as a single from *Love Gun* was the naughty "Christine Sixteen" backed with "Shock Me." The song managed a #25 placement on the Billboard charts, while the second single, "Love Gun" / "Hooligan," stalled at #61. The album as a whole fared much better, reaching #4. But soon it was back to work on a new album, with Kiss, again, striking while the iron was hot, enjoying a year in which a Gallup poll declared them the most popular band in America, outgunning Led Zeppelin, The Eagles, and the band's up-the-coast rivals, Aerosmith.

Gene picked the brothers Van Halen to help him work up a couple of the *Love Gun* demos.

Love Gun tour, London Gardens, London, Ontario, July 18, 1977.

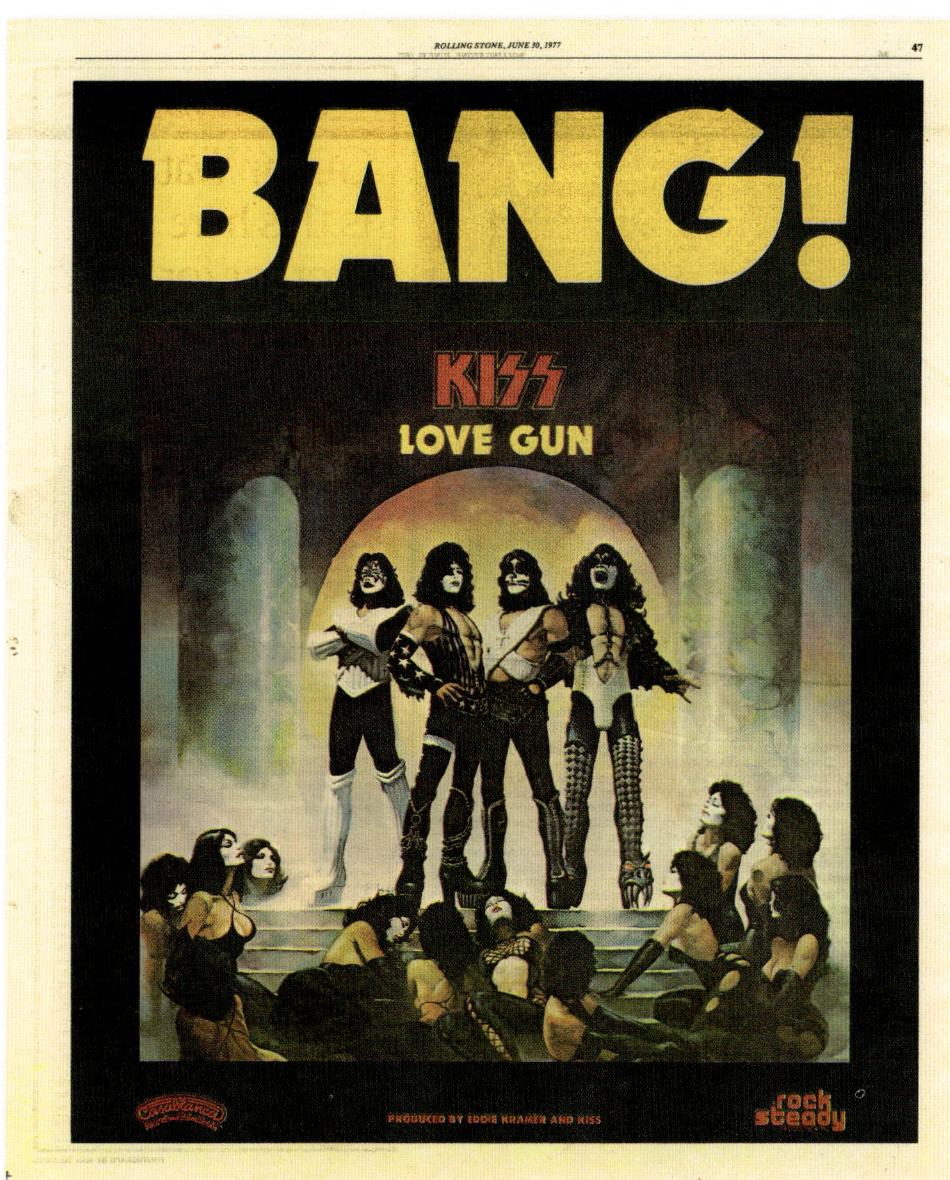
ROLLING STONE, JUNE 30, 1977
47
BANG!
KISS
LOVE GUN
PRODUCED BY EDDIE KRAMER AND KISS
rock steady

& Fun Productions Announce...
KISS
GOOD SEATS STILL AVAILABLE
WITH SPECIAL GUEST STARS
CHEAP TRICK
FRI·SAT·SUN AUG 26, 27, 28
AT THE FABULOUS
FORUM
MANCHESTER & PRAIRIE
ALL SEATS RESERVED: $9.50, 8.50, 7.50
AVAILABLE AT: THE FORUM BOX OFFICE, ALL TICKETRON OUTLETS,
AND ALL MUTUAL AGENCIES
FOR FURTHER INFORMATION CALL
PRODUCED BY FUN PRODUCTIONS/A DAVID FOREST COMPANY

VIP-2566
LOVE GUN
ラブガン／キッス
HOOLIGAN
KISS
¥600

©1977 CASABLANCA RECORD & FILMWORKS, INC.
NBLP 7057
KISS LOVE GUN
KISS LOVE GUN
KISS LOVE GUN
rock steady
rock steady
A   B
KISS
Produced by KISS
& Eddie Kramer
Engineered by:
Eddie Kramer &
Corky Stasiak
for Remarkable
Productions, Inc.
SIDE A
"CHRISTINE SIXTEEN"
(Simmons)
From the Casablanca album
NBLP 7057 "Love Gun"
©1977 Casablanca Record and
FilmWorks, Inc.
STEREO
NB 889
(NB 889 AS RE 1)
Kiss Songs,
Inc. (ASCAP)
Time: 2:52
CRISTINA DIECISEIS
"Christine sixteen" / Simmons
2' 25"
KISS
Kiss Songs, Inc.
P-1977
FABRICADO EN MEXICO POR GAMMA, S.A.
CUBIERTO EL DERECHO DE EJECUCION PUBLICA EN MEXICO

17
DEUCE
ALIVE II

The symmetry was too hard to pass up. Kiss dropped its incendiary *Alive!* device after three studio albums, and now there were three more, all of them perfect for the picking to create two good records out of a trio with weak spots. Only, as it turned out, for *Alive II*, issued on October 14, 1977, the guys would be cherry-picking only half the songs instead of two-thirds, because they'd be saving a side of the album for five brand-new studio tracks. But there had in fact been other ideas. Bill Aucoin had gotten the band's Budokan show recorded on the Japanese campaign and had proposed putting out a live album after *Rock and Roll Over*. But the tapes were deemed inadequate, and instead we got *Love Gun*.

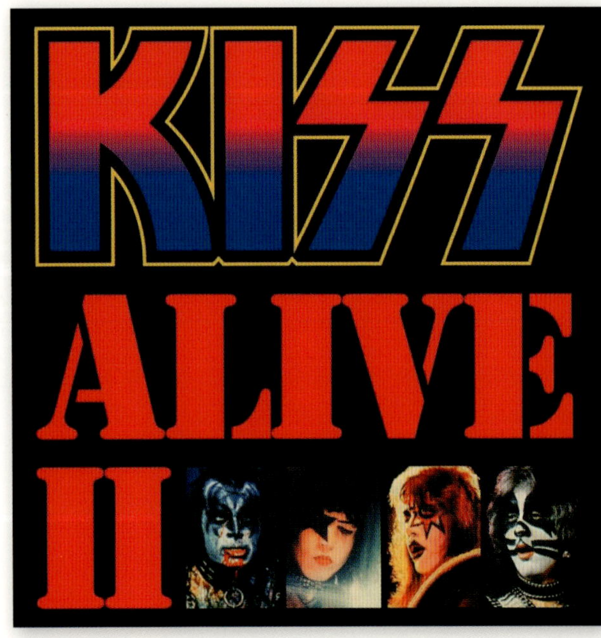

Math and scheduling aside, fans loved *Alive II*, sending the record double platinum within a month, en route to a double platinum standing, achieved in 1996. The three previous records had definite highlights, making sides one, two, and three robust. Side one packed the biggest heavy metal punch, with a lone track, "Ladies Room," stopping it from being a complete onslaught. Side two featured three singles and a crowd favorite in Ace's "Shock Me." Side four is back to the heavy levels of side one, save for the necessary "Beth." Throughout, there's an excitement, achieved through crowd noise, loose drumming, and increased tempos and aggression.

Much of the material hails from the band's shows at The Forum in Los Angeles on August 26, 27, and 28, 1977, but they did rescue a couple of songs from Japan, namely "Beth" and "I Want You." As well, a couple of songs—"Hard Luck Woman" and "Tomorrow and Tonight"—come from the Capitol Theatre sessions in Passaic, New Jersey, where they recorded live without a crowd to produced the bed tracks for the studio side of the album.

As for side four, those tracks were started at the Capitol Theatre with ensemble playing and finished at Electric Lady. An undisputed highlight is heavy metal monster "Rocket Ride," written by Ace and Sean Delaney and sung by Ace, who also plays all the guitars and bass. Then there's the riffy opener "All American Man," sung by Paul, and "Larger Than Life," sung by Gene, both songs neatly autobiographical and well regarded by fans. "Rockin' in the U.S.A." is a bit of a throwaway, as is the cover of the Dave Clark Five's "Any Way You Want It," which feels like a follow-up to "Then She Kissed Me."

For the cover art, the band created something that was both curiously exciting and corporate at once. Huge lettering dominates over four small individual headshots. The same headshots repeat on the back. The gatefold presents the stage in all of its fiery glory (the author saw this show in Montreal on July 12, Cheap Trick supporting), along with credits. The inner sleeves present another skipped opportunity—first off, they are the same and then one side shows pictures of the previous albums with the other being a blurry crowd shot. There is, however, a merchandise order form, a die-cut decal set, and an eight-page photo booklet.

All told, *Alive II* was a success. Not only did its live material meet the visceral standard set by *Alive!*, with respect to sequencing, pacing, and simple songs sounding bold and hard-hitting live, but side four stood up to any of the previous six sides of studio material, perhaps side one of *Destroyer* excepted. Worrying, however, was that a session guitarist, Bob Kulick, had been collared to play on three of the songs. This would serve as a metaphor for the breakdown of the team dynamic moving forward, until Peter and Ace, one by one, would find themselves out of the band and swiftly replaced.

Alive II-era Kiss in a shot that was also a poster which adorned many a bedroom wall in the late 1970s.

PART TWO
KISS MINOR

Kiss with Japanese
maiko at a press
conference in Tokyo,
March 1978.

18

GOT TO CHOOSE

MEMBERS ISSUE
SOLO ALBUMS

The Kiss "solo albums" feature now-iconic artwork by Eraldo Carugati.

Post-hippie prog-rockers Yes already did this three years earlier, and, as it turned out, did it much better. But of course, Kiss gets all the credit . . . and then all the dreadful notices—there's some karma for you. What we're talking about is when Kiss checked out for a year and emerged by the end of it with four solo albums, all issued on the same day, September 18, 1978, each with matching packaging, including inside a 17" x 22" (43 x 56 cm) (badly) illustrated poster with puzzle edges that match to the next, next, and next guy's picture.

It was an audacious move that turned into a debacle. Paul's record sounded like Kiss lite, which irked fans. Gene's record was half Kiss lite and half easy listening, which maddened fans. Peter's record was a combination of R&B, yacht rock, retro music, and any other type of easy listening that doesn't fit those categories, which enraged fans. Ace, on the other hand, came up with a suite of songs that sounded like a slightly heavier Kiss record from 1976 and 1977, not quite "Shock Me" and "Rocket Ride" in the composite, but on its way. It also coughed up a left-field hit in a cover of Russ Ballard's "New York Groove," made moderately famous by post-glam popsters Hello. The *Ace Frehley* album "satisfied" fans, even if it's ascended through the decades to be seen as some sort of masterpiece.

Two singles were shuffled off to Buffalo from Peter's album, and one each from the others. "New York Groove" was the only hit, reaching #13, with "Radioactive" also causing a mild rash at #47. Gene's album sold best at the time, reaching #22 on the Billboard charts, with Ace's album reaching #26, Paul's #40, and Peter's #43. Ace's record has sold best over time.

The band found itself ridiculed for the material and also for the dodginess of the platinum status gerrymandered for all four of the albums. It's usually one of the first examples chucked and chuckled when people talk about the abuse and manipulation of the RIAA gold and platinum system, with the albums shipping into stores platinum but a substantial number of them being returned over the ensuing months (as the joke goes, "they shipped gold and returned platinum").

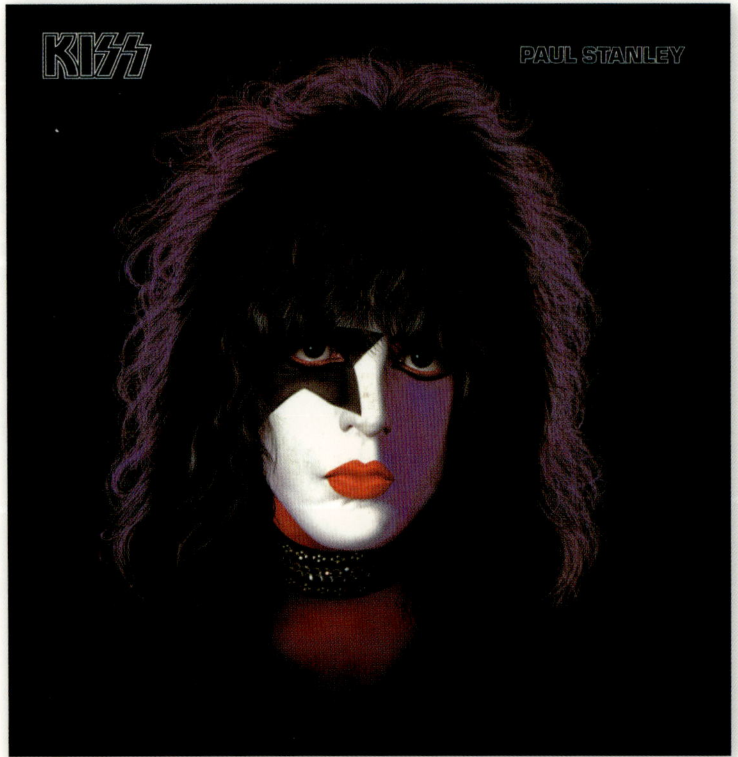

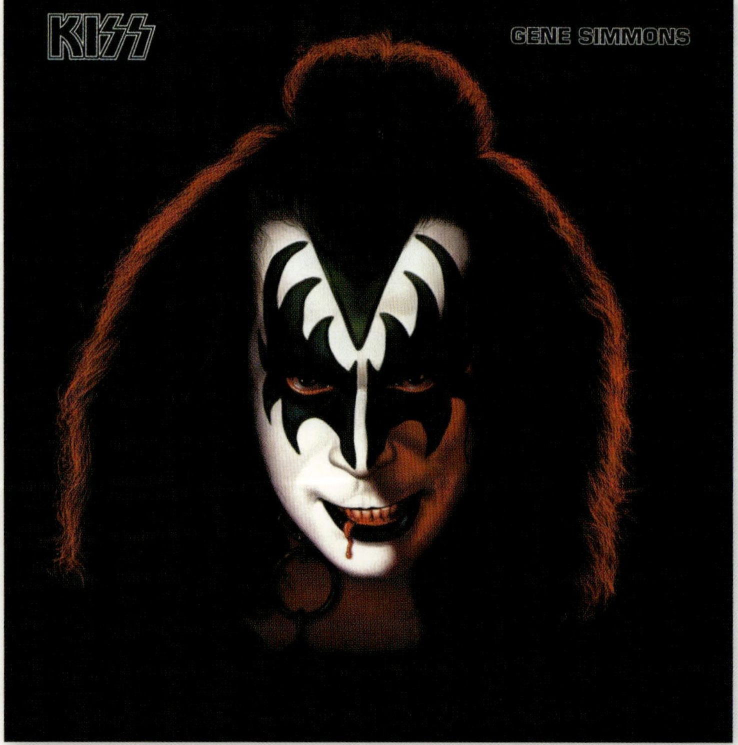

And once platinum status was bestowed, it was never revoked. Free, cheap, deleted, dubious counting, chart manipulation, sent but not ordered . . . all manner of subterfuge was used back in the day, and Casablanca had a reputation for being one of the worst offenders. Plus, the label had spent $2.5 million on promotion, making the sting that much sharper. Neil Bogart was a gambler, and Bill Aucoin and Kiss liked to go big as well. This time it didn't work, and there'd be another embarrassing miscalculation before the year was out.

The biggest hurt was put on the fans by Peter's album. To be sure, Peter was already on his way out of the band, by mutual agreement, but his record caused shocked listeners to reflect that he was living a lie as part of Kiss (in the end, curiosity killed off the cat). Gene's record evoked echoes of this as well. The project might have fared better if these guys had kept their staff lists manageable, but fans had little to sink their teeth into with the dizzying array of no-name musicians (mostly old buddies and studio guys) helping out on the records (one bright spot: there were only three covers in total). Gene had some famous folks, but even that was annoying, because you never got a sense anything amounted to a band, given how everybody is around for a few songs at most, amplified by all the studios visited. Plus, it just felt like a hobnob with stars, with art being the furthest thing from important.

In the end, not one of the records felt like the work of a guy with something to say, or a record made by four pals that might light out on a club tour, maybe even, God forbid, support Kiss, with the Kiss guy doing double duty. In composite, most worrying was the idea that beyond Kiss, nobody in the band was particularly interesting. Is it hyperbole to say that the solo-albums fiasco killed Kiss?

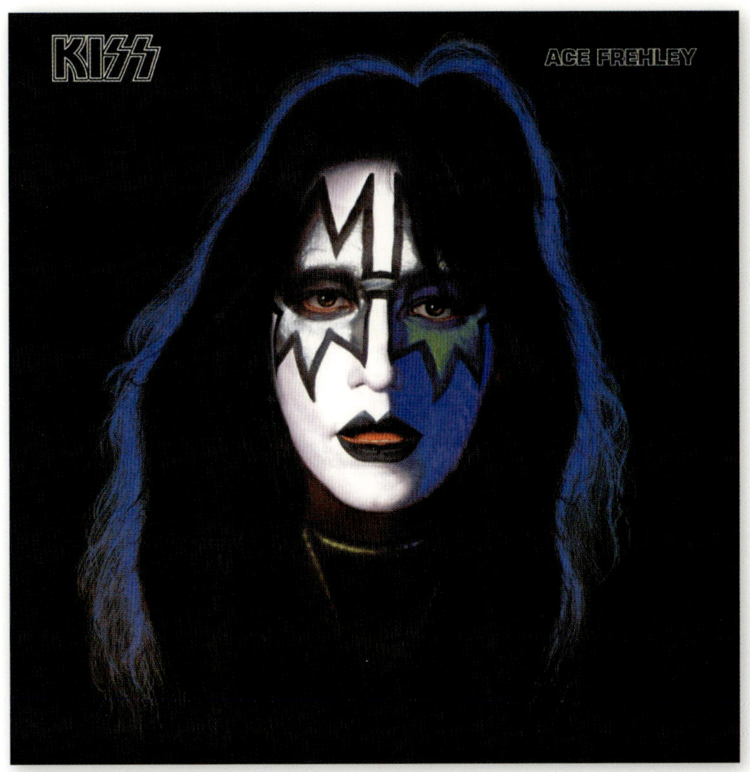

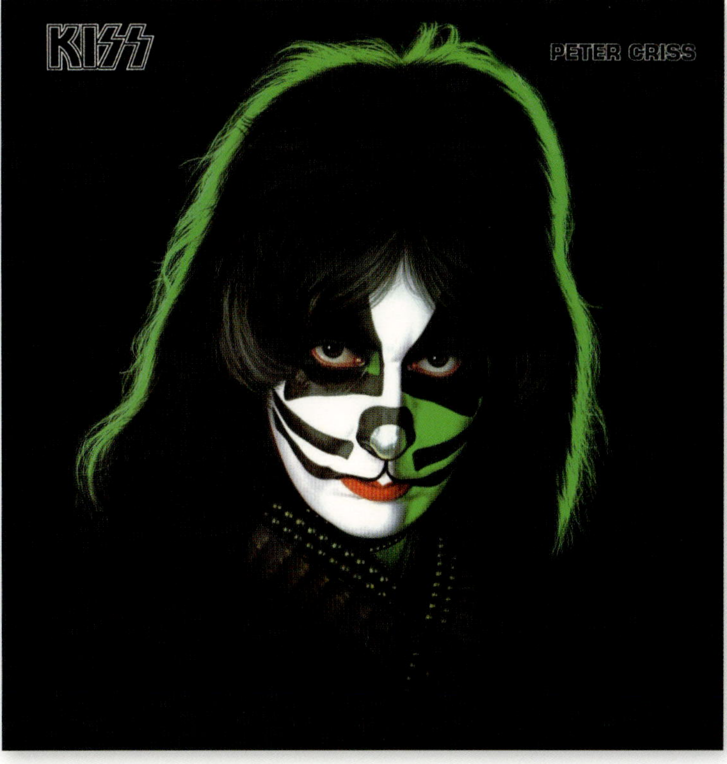

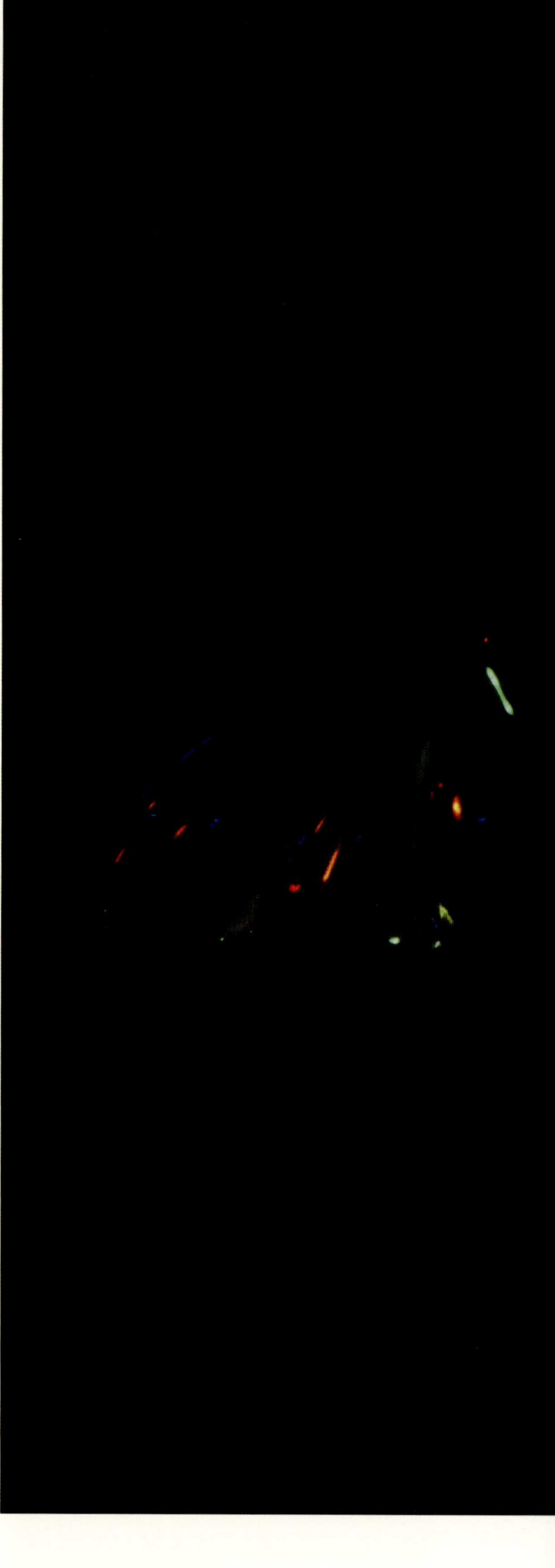

Alive II tour, Olympia
Stadium, Detroit, Michigan,
January 20, 1978.

IS THAT YOU?

KISS MEETS THE PHANTOM OF THE PARK

Gene as "the Demon" in the made-for-TV superhero movie *Kiss Meets the Phantom of the Park.*

Kiss took a holiday from playing live in 1978, working hard in January and mounting a short Japanese tour, but then that was it. The rest of the year was spent getting up to no good, with Ace and Peter drinking and drugging too much and all the guys making solo albums. What they didn't do is learn how to act, getting barely a crash course in the fine art before being tossed into an ill-advised made-for-TV superhero movie called *Kiss Meets the Phantom of the Park*. Produced by Hanna-Barbera, more known for animation, the Kiss film came off like an episode of *Scooby-Doo*—ironically, in 2015 Kiss would star in a Scooby-Doo film bearing a similar plotline.

Tearing through a budget of $3 million, Kiss and crew descended upon the Magic Mountain amusement park in Valencia, California, ill prepared on the acting front and disinterested in the convoluted plot of the movie and thus uninvested and confused scene to scene. As Paul frames it, the guys were barely talking to one another at that point, and both Peter and Ace would often be absent from filming or kick off early, resulting in stunt doubles to be used, which was challenging when Ace's was African American. Acting surly and monosyllabic with writers when the project began, Ace was given hardly any lines and Peter can be heard only during the band's performance of "Beth." Otherwise, he was dubbed over by Michael Bell, who went on to acclaim as the voice of various Smurfs. Gene, on the other hand, was heard mostly through effects, leaving only Paul to say anything reasonably intelligent.

Pitched to the guys as "*A Hard Day's Night* meets *Star Wars*," the plot pits Kiss against mad scientist Abner Devereaux, animatronic Kiss doubles, and some albino monkeys. It seems as if Devereaux is jealous that a Kiss concert is threatening his job, which he is doing poorly, and he mounts a kidnapping scheme along with a plot to destroy Kiss and the park itself. There are talismans in a box that, if stolen, cause Kiss to lose their powers, which amount to laser special effects circa 1978.

The movie aired on October 28, 1978, just in time for Halloween, with the cruel trick of the band's four solo albums now but a month passed in the rearview mirrors of fans and their Kiss-mobiles. After a brief period when the Kiss guys could be heard promising that *Phantom of the Park* represented the start of a brilliant James Bond–like future for the band, they distanced themselves from the project and went years telling staffers never to speak of the movie in their presence.

Indeed, there's a weird congruence to the band doing the movie and the solo albums in the same year, as well as the movie's parallels with how the band was portrayed in the comic book from 1977—in fact, the second one, Marvel Super Special! #5 coincided perfectly with the new projects.

Exactly a year earlier, in an episode of hit sitcom *Happy Days*, Richie Cunningham drives the boat as the Fonz, in his leather jacket and on water skis, hits a ramp and sails over a penned-in shark. This gave rise to the concept of "jumping the shark," coined by Jon Hein in 1985, meaning out of ideas, clutching at straws, being desperate for attention as the brand wanes. Had Hein been a Kiss fan, instead we might have wound up with "... and that's when they put out four solo albums and made a movie."

ACE FOR THE WIN

The core narrative from the 1978 solo albums story is that Ace's proposal was both the best of the four records and, more objectively, the closest to the Kiss canon, the hardest rocking. Amusingly, both of those conjectures have become practically the first utterance from any fan when the subject comes up, followed by "But I really like Paul's too; it's really underrated."

See also our official entry for a quick survey on all four, but our task here is to celebrate the one most celebrated, indeed a record that is also widely the most beloved of Ace's seven albums of fully original solo material to date.

Ace himself acknowledges as much. "Yes, it's true: Most people cite my '78 self-titled *Ace Frehley* solo record with Kiss as their favorite Ace record, and I've tried to take that record apart and figure out what made it tick, to get into the same mind-set as I was back in 1978. I think I've captured some of the same textures on recent albums. But I got a good vibe from that record. I tried to make it as good as possible."

One of the charms of the *Ace Frehley* record is that Ace provides all the lead vocals, unsurprisingly. Also unsurprising is that he plays all the guitars and even most of the bass, with Will Lee playing on three tracks. There are a handful of helpers, but besides Ace, the key collaborators are drummer Anton Fig and producer Eddie Kramer.

"Yes, I used Anton on my first solo album, but I also used him on probably six records until I moved out to California," explains Ace. "One of the best drummers I've ever worked with. I remember when I was gearing up to do that album, I told Eddie I was looking for a drummer and he came back to me with Anton's name. Ironically, I already had his name

through another source. I looked at Eddie and laughed and said, 'That's funny; I was going to bring his name up to you and you tell me about him.' He's a special drummer. He came on a couple Frehley's Comet tours with me, but he has his obligation with David Letterman. We remain good friends.

"As for Eddie, I learned a wealth of knowledge from Eddie Kramer, as far as EQing guitars, the way you mic a Marshall cabinet or a Fender cabinet, different combinations of mics. You know, use a '57 and a ribbon mic and they blend together nicely. That way you have more control over the sound and can alter it a little, just by changing the blend of the two microphones. Track a Les Paul and then overdub it with a Fender. Fenders have a different harmonic range, so when you blend the two together you get a thicker sound. Little tricks like that. Ways to record an acoustic and ways not to record an acoustic. Me and Eddie used to experiment a lot. That's why I always loved to work with him."

One hears this blend of acoustic and electric on "Ozone" and "What's on Your Mind?," with Ace crediting Pete Townshend for this type of arrangement. "Yeah, I would have found invariably that he has an acoustic tossed under the electric, and that's something I've been doing since this first solo record. The secret to doing that is playing the same part on the acoustic, but just tuck it down in the mix so that you really don't hear it that much, but if you take it away, you miss it. But Pete Townshend is probably one of the greatest rhythm guitar players of all time. He can play the same chord in twenty different positions on the neck. By idolizing these guys and studying the way they put songs together, that's how I learned to do it.

"I was doing that first album in Upstate New York," continues Ace. "We had rented out the Colgate Estate, right down the street from Lime Rock speedway, and we brought in what was essentially a studio inside a truck. Basically, we just set up at this empty estate, drums and guitars and amplifiers everywhere, to get like natural reverb sounds. I remember cutting acoustic guitars in a wood study. I had an amplifier in a marble bathroom. Eddie Kramer is an old-school producer, so we always went for natural reverb rather than canned stuff. That's why that record is so special. And we were all very level-headed. It was basically me, Eddie Kramer, Anton Fig, and his assistant, and we just locked ourselves away in this mansion. I got away from all the party animals, my crazy friends and drinking buddies, and basically just buckled down and focused on the record because I knew it was going to be an important album in my life."

Of the members' four
1978 solo efforts, Ace
Frehley's was a general-
consensus favorite. Ace
is seen here on the *Alive
II* tour, January 20, 1978,
in Detroit, Michigan.

Ace Frehley has gone
on to release six more
solo albums to boot.
Here he rocks Stuart,
Florida in October 2019.

Ace scored a moderate hit with an errant smudge of poppy glam on the album called "New York Groove," written by Russ Ballard. Elsewhere there's a proggy instrumental and, sure, "Speedin' Back to My Baby" and "What's on Your Mind?" are light fare. But the rest of the album is pretty much a case of stomp that distortion pedal and let's rock, highlights being punky opener "Rip It Out" and "Snow Blind," Ace's favorite song on the album (along with "New York Groove") and pretty much his attempt at Black Sabbath–derived doom metal, which rears its head again on the chorus of side two's "Wiped-Out."

"It has a nice variety of songs," reflects Ace in closing. "It had a cool instrumental, it had a catchy hit single, it had the heavy rockers. I mean, those three elements right there are enough for me. You can never go back in time, but you can listen to what you did and try to figure out what made it special and try to capture that again. I felt I had something to prove, and when I feel that way, I'm fired up. It was like, 'I'll show you.' Because prior to going into the studio, Paul and Gene kind of made a comment to me that, you know, if I needed any help, don't hesitate to give them a call. But I took it more as a sarcastic remark. I walked out of the meeting saying to myself, 'I'll show you what I can do on my own,' you know? Afterward, they didn't even want to acknowledge it. I think there might have been a bit of jealousy, but who knows? I think Gene, to this day, will say that his record sold more than mine. But they're always trying to rewrite history. Go figure (laughs)."

Dynasty tour, Hollywood Sportatorium, Pembrooke Pines, Florida, June 17, 1979.

20

I WAS MADE FOR LOVIN' YOU

DYNASTY

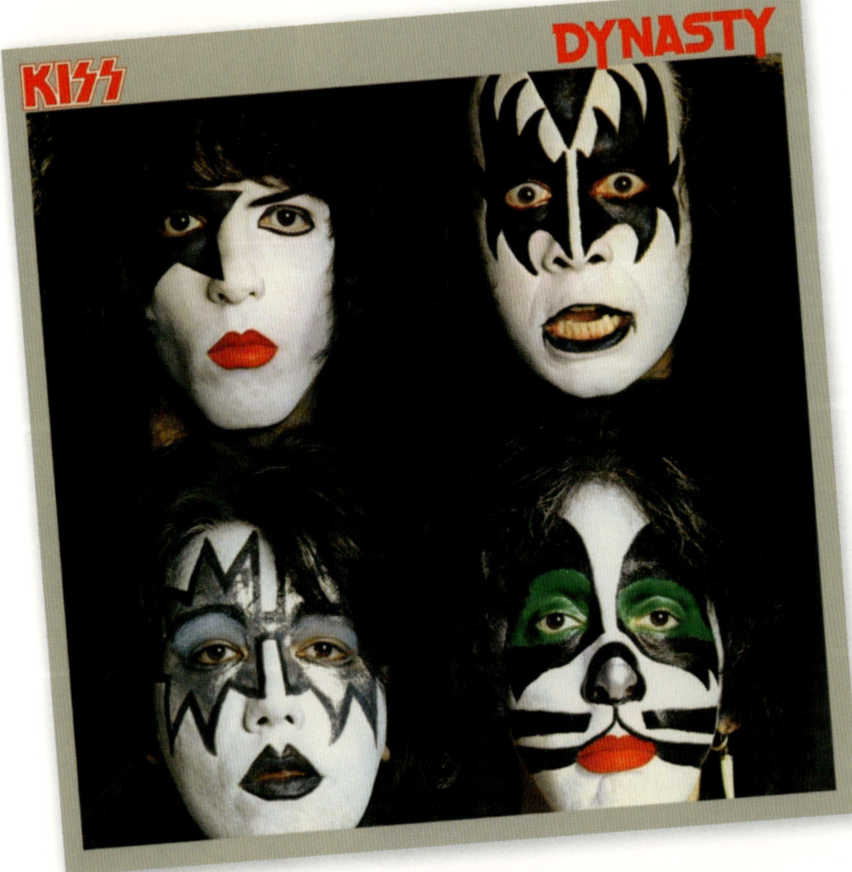

Two years on from *Love Gun* we got "the return of Kiss," as it was billed, when in fact we got an evolved Kiss, a fractured Kiss, and a disco Kiss—granted, it was only one song (well, maybe two), but "I Was Made for Loving You" was so dominant, it's all anybody outside of Kissworld recalls about the album. With its catchy title, *Dynasty* (released on May 23, 1979) offered equally crisp cover art, which features the classic lineup, even though Peter only plays on one track, having been deemed unworkable by producer Vini Poncia due to his substance abuse issues (Peter had also injured his hand in a car accident). Ironically, Poncia had entered the orbit of the band by producing Peter's solo album.

Back on the subject of disco, people also forget that the album in total is fairly close in heaviness to the previous three, with most of the power-chording buried on side two. Still, there's more experimentation, which makes sense when you find out that the guys were at odds with one another and working alone on demos. As well, causing more distinction track to track, the guys tended to play most of the instruments on the songs that they brought in.

Peter had the unlikable "Dirty Livin'" accepted from his four—it's the only song he drums on and it's the only song he sings. Gene is credited on only two songs, "Charisma" and "X-Ray Eyes," which are also the only two songs he sings. Paul sings on the three songs he wrote. The almost-disco "Sure Know Something," a cowrite with Poncia, was issued as a single but stalled at #47, while "Magic Touch" is an underrated gem that would have fit on Paul's solo album. "I Was Made for Loving You" had Paul writing with Poncia and disco-enabler Desmond Child. To be sure, scandalously, it's disco, but it's also kind of rocking and has sophisticated chord changes.

"Yadda yadda yadda," laughs Ace, asked for his views on it. "I didn't particularly like that one (laughs). A disco rock song. Actually, when I first heard it, I was like, 'I don't even want to get involved with this song,' even though it became one of our biggest hits, more outside of the United States than inside of the United States, from what I understand. We gained new fans when that song became a hit, but I think we also lost some of the hardcore heavy metal fans who were turned off by it. But music is a double-edged sword."

In fact, it's Ace to the rescue (as it was with the solo album project and side four of *Alive II*), with the Spaceman writing two songs and singing three—it's also Ace's solo album drummer, Anton Fig, who deputized on the album for Peter. From the Stones' *Their Satanic Majesties Request*, "2000 Man" was the band's most inspired cover choice since "Kissin' Time," and Ace sings it like a punk rocker, even though punk was dead by 1979. "Hard Times" and "Save Your Love," again, near the end of the album, are the two hardest-rocking songs on *Dynasty* and arguably the best, along with, yes, "I Was Made for Loving You."

As Ace alludes to, the band's novelty dance track was a huge hit worldwide, dragging the album up the charts with it. Back home, the album quickly went platinum, granted and hit #9 on the Billboard charts, partly due to the single but also due to pent-up demand for "the return of Kiss."

Backstage at the Hollywood Sportatorium in Florida, June 17, 1979.

This page and opposite: The *Dynasty* era saw an infusion of color into the band's wardrobe. Sportatorium, Pembrooke Pines, Florida, June 17, 1979.

Belkin
PRODUCTIONS
Presents
KISS
Cheap Trick
Cheap Trick
& special guest
FRIDAY
JULY 13
8:00 P.M.
Pontiac Silverdome
POZER
Detroit Rock City!

21

WHEN YOUR WALLS COME DOWN

APPEARANCE ON THE *TOMORROW* SHOW DOESN'T GO WELL

NBC broadcast legend Tom Snyder responded with aplomb during the band's wild Halloween 1979 appearance on his show.

Following up their Halloween 1976 appearance with Paul Lynde, Kiss showed up on the late-night *Tomorrow* with Tom Snyder on October 31, 1979, only this time all four of the guys would have to sit down and participate in a half-hour conversation with the professional and likable talk show veteran.

After a long, scripted introduction to the band, which included a clip from *Phantom of the Park* and a sampling from loud live versions of "Sure Know Something" and "I Was Made for Loving You," out came Kiss, decked out in their over-the-top *Dynasty* costumes, which, as history would have it, represented another example of Kiss jumping the shark.

Ace admits to being nervous before the show and drinking vodka in the car on the way into the city, and once at the studio, Bill Aucoin had Champagne at the ready. But it's a stretch to say that he comes off as inebriated. To be sure, he laughs louder and heartier than the other guys and interrupts Gene, who throws him daggers. But without knowing the story, you'd come away from the show thinking he was just the goofier guy onstage, with most of the wisecracks and cackles. Frankly, with him loosening things up, it looks like they are getting along. Plus, it's Paul who starts talking about underage girls, and Gene, with his disapproving looks, also makes things awkward. The only hiccup in Ace's story about throwing furniture out the window at a hotel in Arkansas is when he mentions drugs, which Snyder quickly "corrects." Ace also takes his armbands off and puts them on Snyder's teddy bear, which he then sits on his knee like a dutiful mother for the rest of the show.

When all is said and done, the worst part of the experience is that Paul and Gene knew Ace was lit up and they took offense to that, as a show of disrespect to the fans as well as putting the band's reputation in jeopardy on live national TV. The *Dynasty* tour, which had seen poor ticket sales, would be over in six weeks, with Peter not playing with the band again until the reunion. Ace was working on a slow exit as well, with his hijacking of the Snyder appearance—as mild, good-natured, and entertaining as it was—representing another ill-advised irritant to an irked Paul and Gene.

Snyder, for his part, did great, rolling with the punches and indicating afterward in the dressing room that he enjoyed himself. Indeed, very little of it is awkward, and for the few quips that sink like a lead balloon, well, those are spread evenly among Ace, Paul, and Gene, with Peter being the only one who gets out of the situation unscathed, comments on his gun collections and wanting to be a 1920s gangster notwithstanding.

The band supporting *Dynasty* in Albuquerque, New Mexico, a few weeks after the Snyder appearance. The cape motif made the guys look cumbersome, like they snagged the drapery on the way out of their hotel rooms.

22

TWO SIDES OF THE COIN

UNMASKED

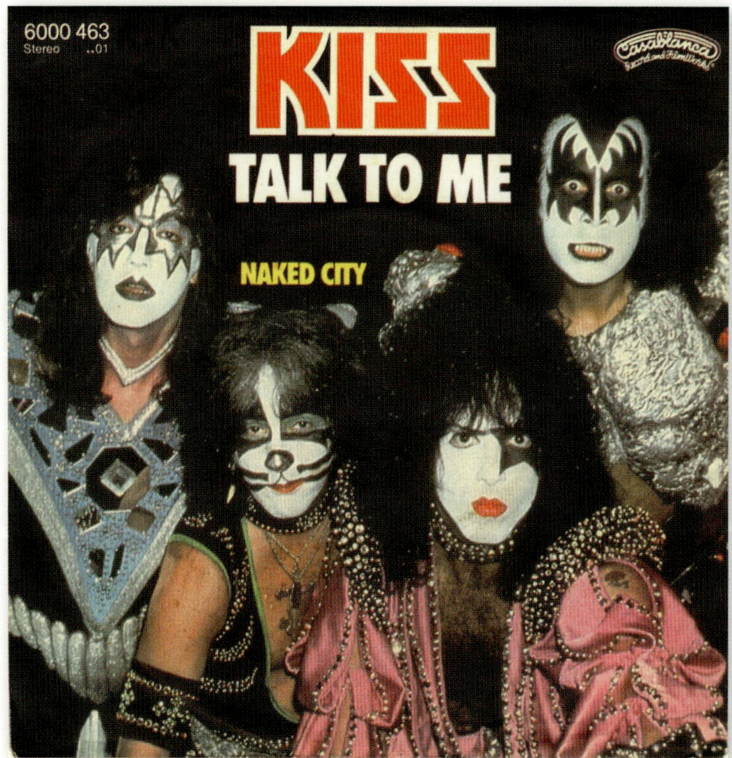

Gene and Paul were kind of right—for five minutes anyway—that hard rock was on the outs, and that pop might be the way to go. The success of the band's dance hit, somewhat at home but enticingly worldwide, purred as much, as did the steep decline in the fortunes of every fellow heavy rock act from the '70s precisely in 1979 (save for Van Halen, who were new). So, when Vini Poncia suggested they lighten up on the Slade *Alive!* buffalo burger boogie rock and get with the times, they agreed.

On the other hand, Ace resisted, and therefore needed further placating. In conjunction with Peter's drug issues and attendant drumming abilities getting worse, they decided once more to use Anton Fig, the drummer from Ace's solo album, therefore ascribing to Ace a subtle nudging that he mattered.

Unmasked, recorded at the beginning of 1980 at the Record Plant and issued on May 20, would be the result. The cover art telegraphed that we shouldn't expect a proper unmasking, but fans still thought there'd be something inside that proved them wrong. Instead, there was a poster that rubbed it in, featuring an enlargement of the same illustration from the front, revealing that the band looked the same under their masks.

Already ticked off, what pimply purchasers found inside was an album about as weighty as Gene's or Paul's solo albums, with a boy/girl feel closer to Paul's and even Peter's. In fact, at the writing end, it's producer Poncia who is in on seven of eleven tracks, and the other guys are all busted up, flummoxed, working again on their own, doing what they did last time, making their own demos and then playing on their own songs. Most significantly, this is because Gene and Paul were on the outs with Ace, who gamely contributes "Talk to Me," "Two Sides of the Coin," and "Torpedo Girl," the three most Kiss-like, fan-friendly songs on the record. Ace sings all three as well, with Simmons singing another three and Paul five. The next heaviest track is opener "Is That You?," provided by outside writer Gerald McMahon, soon to find fame as a penner of songs for movies. So, the record opens promising, but then we get to the prechorus and suddenly Kiss become a soul band, and

Arriving at London's
Heathrow Airport from
Milan, Italy, September
1980. Manager Bill Aucoin
is behind the band.

Ace pulls a classic
guitar face while
playing his cherryburst
Les Paul on the
Dynasty tour.

then to the chorus, which is heavy enough, but happier than the verse, a clear indication that the guys are thinking differently.

Issued as lead single was "Shandi," an easy listening shocker with even less rock to it than "I Was Made for Loving You," and oddly less apt as a Kiss song than "Beth" and "Hard Luck Woman." Yet like last year's hit, the song was a left-field success in some pretty faraway countries, prompting tour dates that took the band to Europe and Australia only, with North America left off the slate entirely.

To be fair, "Shandi" was about as weird as it got, with the balance of the album in possession of mostly the same arrangements as other Kiss albums, save for the odd synth line an' lick from Poncia and backing vocals that are jarringly saccharine. The overriding difference is a sort of new wave and hard pop mind-set to the melodies and lyrics, along with production from Poncia that lacks bottom end. In other words, the fuzz pedal is still the main effect, but the songs sound like that of a different band, one younger and yet more conservative, eager to please radio programmers, the right age but not hip, like John Cougar or Tom Petty, or Hall & Oates (if they were the right age).

Kiss fans were not pleased. *Unmasked* went gold on curiosity alone and never further, with none of the three singles meaning anything at home. Even given the glasses through which anything from the band eventually and famously looks rosier, the reputation of *Unmasked* has not significantly improved. Gene and Paul both disown the album, with only Ace plumping for its songs, perceptively blaming the failure of the record on the production. It's more than that (like I say, a mind-set), but to be sure, *Unmasked* is only a handful of decisions away from *Rock and Roll Over* and *Love Gun* and even less away from *Dynasty*, point being that Kiss had been leaning this way for a while.

23

FITS LIKE A GLOVE

ERIC CARR'S FIRST SHOW WITH KISS

After a curious episode where Peter showed up at a rehearsal with a music stand, claiming he had changed his ways and even learned how to read music (he hadn't), it was decided that he wasn't going to cut it moving forward. Ace had to be persuaded, causing more friction, with the guys conducting auditions and settling on Paul Caravello.

Because Kiss mischievously did not "unmask" in conjunction with their new *Unmasked* album, they needed someone unknown. Eric fit the bill, having played with working bands around New York for more than ten years but not recording, joining Kiss at thirty years old. At his audition, not only did he sing, but he had also studied up for the tryouts and was more familiar than the guys were with respect to how the harmonies were stacked on the studio versions of the songs. He was the last to audition but pretty quickly secured the gig.

The band announced the new hire on a syndicated show called *Kids Are People Too*, with Eric "The Fox" Carr calling it "a dream come true." The guys submit to a long interrogation from the show's host as well as kids in the crowd, escaping the situation without embarrassment. One of them even asks why Peter left the band, with Gene replying that he'd gotten himself a new wife. Carr also shows up in the lip-synched live videos of "Talk to Me" and "She's So European," with Peter's last link to the band being the proper production promo clip for the album's first single, "Shandi."

Eric's first show was a warm-up gig on July 25, 1980, at The Palladium, chosen for sentimental reasons, given that it was the location of the band's first industry showcase back in 1973 when it was called The Academy of Music. A coworker of Eric's spotted his parents at the gig, but they covered up by improbably claiming to be there as fans of the band. This would serve as the only *Unmasked* tour date in America, with the band playing from the album "Is That You?," "Talk to Me," and "You're All That I Want." Notably, "Shandi" wasn't in the set list but "New York Groove" and "2000 Man" were, with Gene and Paul striving to keep Ace happy and part of the team.

Then it was off to Europe for a lavish tour that outspent what it brought in, followed by the band's first trip to Australia and New Zealand, where the promoter spared no expense keeping the guys happy, with a swimming pool, mini golf, and games room at every venue. There were private planes stocked with Dom Perignon, and the band and their huge entourage stayed at the best hotels. Relentlessly promoted (and also heavily discounted), *Unmasked* eventually sold more than two hundred thousand copies, with the concerts selling well but not selling out. There was also all manner of Kiss merchandise produced by outside vendors, with a few horror stories of trinkets left unsold. There was a meeting with the mayor of Sydney and a lavish arrival party at the airport. Kiss accountant Chris Lendt said that the band played to 250,000 fans and grossed $3 million. And yet in the end, given the out-of-control spending (including $2 million just on promotion), apparently, as had happened in Europe, the tour lost money.

All told, the two trips represented legendary milestone events for Gene, Paul, and Ace, let alone Eric, given that the band usually played to the Rust Belt. As well, in typical Kiss fashion, they were frantically spending their way through bad times, lavishing upon their fans (as well as themselves) money they no longer had. It was a near-surreal welcome to the excessive end of the music business for a guy that in the weeks after he got the gig, was still going out on calls doing stove repairs.

The band welcomes new drummer Eric Carr to the fold, 1980.

24

DARK LIGHT
MUSIC FROM THE ELDER
CONCEPT ALBUM

ECHOING THEIR RESPONSE TO *KISS MEETS THE PHANTOM OF THE PARK*, THE GUYS WERE PRETTY MUCH INSTANTLY EMBARRASSED BY THE OUTCOME. FANS WEREN'T HAPPY EITHER . . . THE RESULTS WERE SEEN AS WHOLLY INCONGRUOUS WITH THE BAND'S THUS FAR RELENTLESS PARTY-EVERY-DAY HAPPY-MAKING.

Following upon a couple of comic books, a movie, a suite of four solo albums, a disco hit, and a pop album, Kiss always found new ways to jump the shark. *Music from the Elder* is yet another provocation, even if, on paper, creating the band's first concept album after eight records seemed like a good idea, indeed, something the fans might have asked for had they been polled.

The plot of the record arose from a short story from Gene about a boy bestowed superpowers and hero status by the elders to reset the power balance after a period of too much darkness. Fortunately for us, there's only one brief spot of narration, with much else tracked but then removed. Neither here nor there was the fact that the song sequencing was shuffled by the label to showcase the band's most heavy metal song to date, "The Oath," and the pick for lead single, the dour, soft, and unlikable "A World Without Heroes." Typical of concept albums, there are instrumentals as well as progressive rock flourishes and symphonic arrangements, executed by Bob Ezrin and Michael Kamen.

The project began at Ace's state-of-the-art underground studio upstate from Manhattan in Wilton, Connecticut. From there it went to Bob Ezrin's studio compound on a farm north of Toronto, where Bob, admittedly bad with the cocaine at that time, worked to create a combination of *Destroyer* and *The Wall*, which he had just finished for Pink Floyd, resulting in permanent psychological scarring. Notably, Ace wasn't along for the trip to Canada, which ticked him off. Not only were plans being scrapped to make a straight-ahead rock album—working titles included *Disguise the Limit*, *All American Guise*, *Ear Openers*, *In the Flesh*, and *Higher Ground*—but decisions were being made left and right without his say,

Studio performance, 1981. Ace was the first to cut his hair, but Paul was even more ahead of the curve, revealing a nascent hair metal look.

with Eric not being particularly involved either, having been signed up as an employee and not a card-carrying member of Kiss. A couple of Ace's guitar solos got cut in the process as well, plus Ace sings on only one track, "Dark Light," one of the great Kiss songs of all time, cowritten by Ace, Gene, Lou Reed, and Anton Fig, who supplied the catchy yet thoughtful riff.

As Ace told me, "I always pushed for the heaviest songs, and I think it's pretty apparent when you listen to Kiss songs—or listen to Kiss after I left—that I was completely dead-set against the *Elder* album. All through the whole recording process I was telling Paul that I didn't think the direction of it was heavy enough and strong enough, because I just didn't think that's what was going on in music at the time. And it turned out to be the least successful Kiss album."

Echoing their response to *Kiss Meets the Phantom of the Park*, the guys were pretty much instantly embarrassed by the outcome. Fans weren't happy either. Outside of "The Oath," "Dark Light," "I," and "Mr. Blackwell," the results were seen as pretentious and overly serious, wholly incongruous with the band's thus far relentless party-every-day happy-making. A few TV appearances happened, but there was no tour—all the better, given Gene's and Paul's weirdo close-cropped hairstyles and the attendant paring back of the costumes, not that we needed to see any more capes.

Later CD reissues restored the running order, and if anything it made the record worse, front-ending it with the symphonic rock and ponderous balladry of "Fanfare," "Just a Boy," and the egregiously theatrical "Odyssey." No amount of gerrymandering with the rack jobbers could coax the RIAA to certify the album as gold, and it remains uncertified to this day, as does the "blockbuster film" *Music from the Elder* was supposed to portend.

25
I LOVE IT LOUD
CREATURES OF THE NIGHT

I'd say it was a time of transition for Kiss, but the fact is, the band had been in a constant state of flux for four years at this point. The newest life events had the band saying goodbye to Casablanca label founder Neil Bogart, who succumbed to cancer on May 8, 1982. Casablanca had been sold to Polygram, and Kiss signed a new deal, with *Creatures of the Night*, issued on October 28, 1982, being a transitional Casablanca/Polygram item en route to the band's records bearing the Mercury imprint.

Lots of drama inside the band as well, with Ace Frehley out of the band and yet appearing on the album cover, having been replaced by Vinnie Vincent, who provides lead guitar on six of nine tracks, augmented by Robben Ford on two and Steve Farris on one. Weirdly, updated covers exist with Vinnie (these are pirated copies from South America) as well as officially a sans-makeup Kiss lineup with Bruce Kulick as second banana guitarist. Of note, Bruce's brother Bob indeed recorded with the band on some *Creatures* sessions, but none of his material made the record. Conversely, Bob would figure prominently on the four new songs recorded for international hits pack *Killers*, issued in June 1982 to mitigate the commercial failure of *Elder*.

In any event, *Creatures of the Night* also served as the coming-out party for drummer Eric Carr, who had a big hand in transforming the band into a heavy metal machine for the '80s. Unlike Peter or Anton Fig, he's boomy and busy, percussively speaking the language of the New Wave of British heavy metal, the '70s hard rock bands suddenly doing well with a new commercial brand of heavy metal, and also telegraphing the pounds an' sounds of the first wave of hair metal bands about to do significant business in 1983 and 1984.

Gene and Paul are running right beside him, tacking on an outside cowriter or two for each song and winding up with an uncompromising collection of grinding hard rockers forged from a different mind-set from anything heavy Kiss had done before, save for "The Oath" and maybe "Escape from the Island" from the last record.

Prescient of the good times on the Sunset Strip to come, "Keep Me Comin'" is more Poison than Aerosmith but funky like both, while "I Still Love You" is the band's first rote power ballad, really a blueprint for the idea. Elsewhere, "War Machine" is doom, "Creatures of the Night" is an old-timer's version of speed metal but action-packed all the same, and "I Love It Loud" plays to the band's penchant for the anthemic, but, again, competitive with anything we might hear up in the latter half of the decade.

The Michael James Jackson production job is a little boxy, which is something that will plague the band throughout the rest of the decade as well, but all told, *Creatures of the Night* provides a sense of "Kiss is back," despite there being a couple of clunkers, most notably "Saint and Sinner" and "Rock and Roll Hell." The fact that the album didn't certify as gold until 1994, however, proves that goodwill for the band was mostly spent, after three records ill received by Kiss purists. But unlike, say, *Unmasked* or *Peter Criss*, this is a record now highly regarded by the base, as well as the band, who have regularly included "I Love It Loud" and "War Machine" in set lists, along with, to a lesser extent, "Creatures of the Night" and "I Still Love You."

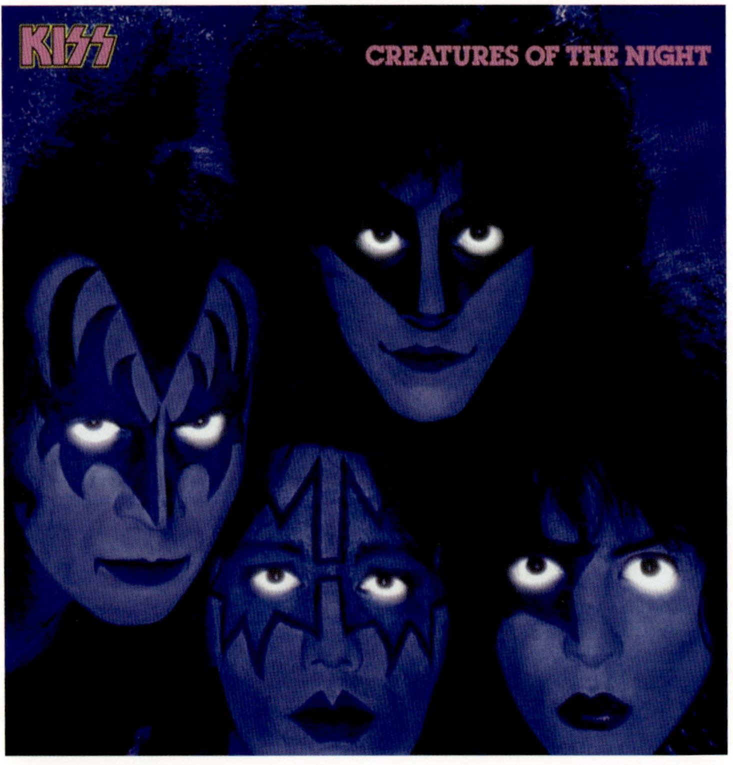

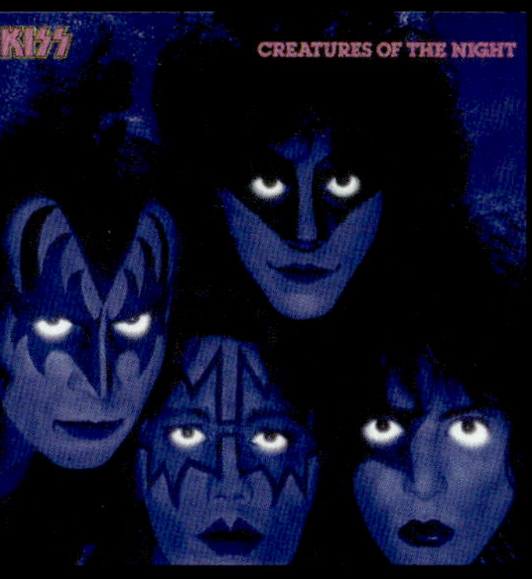

1982
Creatures of the Night
October 28

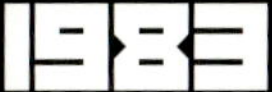
1983
Lick It Up **features new guitarist Vinnie Vincent**
September 22

1984
Animalize **features new guitarist Mark St. John**
September 13

1985
Asylum **features new guitarist Bruce Kulick**
September 16

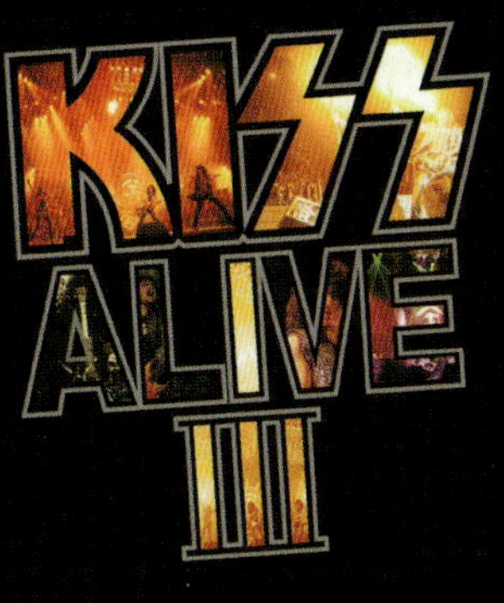

1993
Back to the well with *Alive III*
May 18

1994
First Official Worldwide Kiss Convention
June 17

1995
Kiss perform on *MTV Unplugged*
October 31

1997
Carnival of Souls: The Final Sessions
October 28

2003
Peter Criss performs for the last time with Kiss
December 20

2006
Kiss honored at the first *VH1 Rock Honors*
May 25

2006
Gene Simmons Family Jewels **premiers on A&E**
August 7

2009
Sonic Boom **features new guitarist Tommy Thayer**
October 6

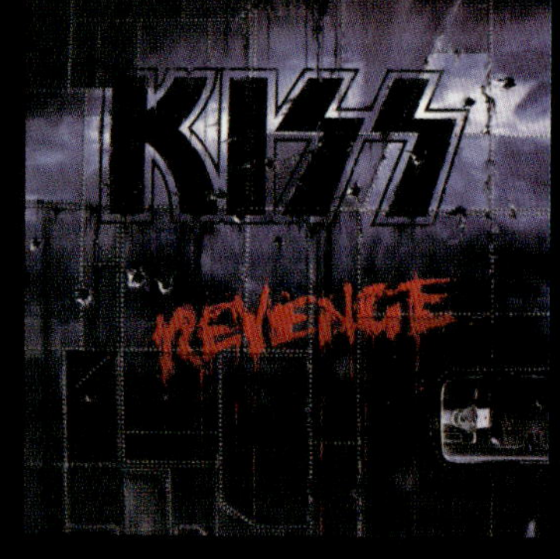

1987
Crazy Nights
September 21

1989
Hot in the Shade
October 17

1991
Eric Carr succumbs to cancer
November 24

1992
Revenge, with new drummer Eric Singer
May 19

1998
Classic-era lineup issues _Psycho Circus_
September 22

1999
Kiss perform at Super Bowl XXXIII
January 31

1999
Kiss-themed feature film _Detroit Rock City_
August 13

2001
The Box Set
November 20

2003
Going classical with _Kiss Symphony: Alive IV_
July 22

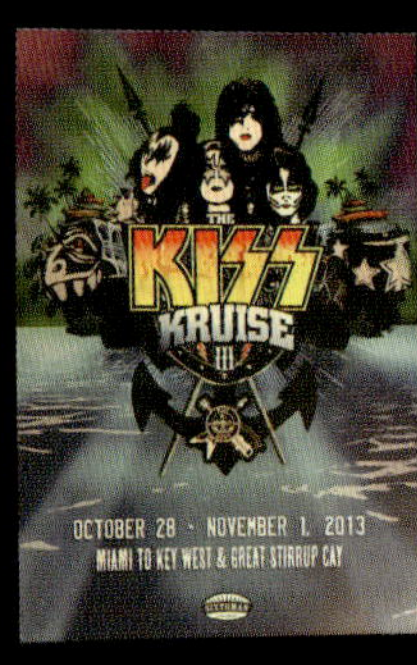

2011
Kiss launch first _Kiss Kruise_
October 13

2012
Monster
October 9

2014
Induction into the Rock & Roll Hall of Fame
April 10

2015
Setting mark for most gold records by an American band
September 15

2019
Kiss embark on _End of the Road World Tour_
January 31

Soon the game of deception that the band had been playing with fans as well as the record company would come crashing down. Ace had been boozing as heavily as ever, and now, after a car accident (mind you, seven months earlier!), there were painkillers involved as well. As he admitted to Paul, he was on the verge of a nervous breakdown. Ace appeared in the "I Love It Loud" video, at press conferences, and on TV stages in Europe miming to songs, but by the time the guys got back from the overseas promotional tour, he'd be out of the picture, replaced by Vinnie Vincent. Now fans had two new painted faces to contend with, resulting in venues averaging 59 percent full across America in early 1983 for the band's expensive military tank–themed show. Kiss were in desperate need of a hit, and fortunately for them, another big anthem, written by Paul and the new guy, was lurking just around the corner.

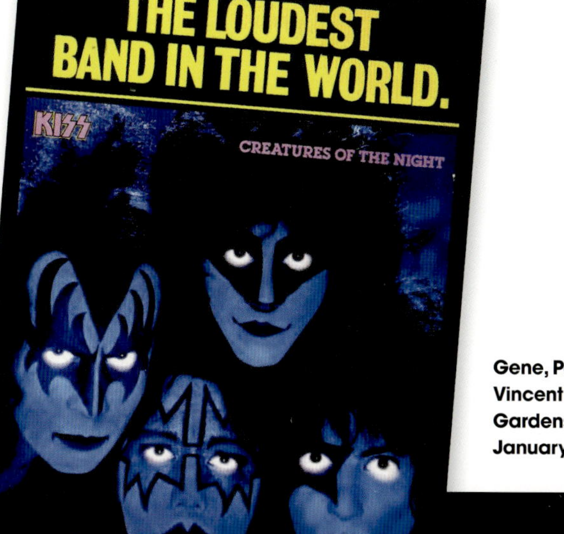

Gene, Paul, and Vinnie Vincent at Maple Leaf Gardens, Toronto, Ontario, January 14, 1983.

PART THREE
MTV, HAIR METAL, AND KISS

Gene, Paul, and Bruce Kulick at Madison Square Garden, New York City, December 16, 1985.

26

NAKED CITY

LICK IT UP, FEATURING NEW GUITARIST VINNIE VINCENT

With Paul griping that the ignored *Creatures of the Night* was every bit as good as the new record, Kiss had another plan to push the new album over the top: removing the makeup. Smartly, they enlisted MTV to help them out, with video jock J.J. Jackson making a big show of it on an extended segment five days before the release of the album. It was a great idea, giving the powerful new music video station the scoop, because in the end, it was MTV that made *Lick It Up* a success. The band cooked up a couple of iconic, signature rock videos for the album's two very strong singles, "Lick It Up" and "All Hell's Breakin' Loose," and the station dutifully aired them, albeit in medium and light rotation. Still, the new-look band came across ready an' willing an' photogenic enough to compete with the likes of Mötley Crüe, Quiet Riot, and Ratt. Kiss came across as a bunch of eye-winking old tarts, golden-age entertainers dressed like Christmas trees, evidently having no problem pulling all the same video vixens as the upstart California bands.

For his part, Eric was thrilled that a song he'd had a big hand in writing, "All Hell's Breakin' Loose," became the album's second single and afterward a huge Kiss anthem forevermore. Amusingly, he was horrified that Paul planned to do a mild rap with the vocal, but in the end realized it was a brilliant move. On the other hand, Eric was not happy with how generous Gene and Paul were with Vinnie Vincent's writing credits, given his own abilities and participation in the process, not to mention the fact that he was no longer the new guy.

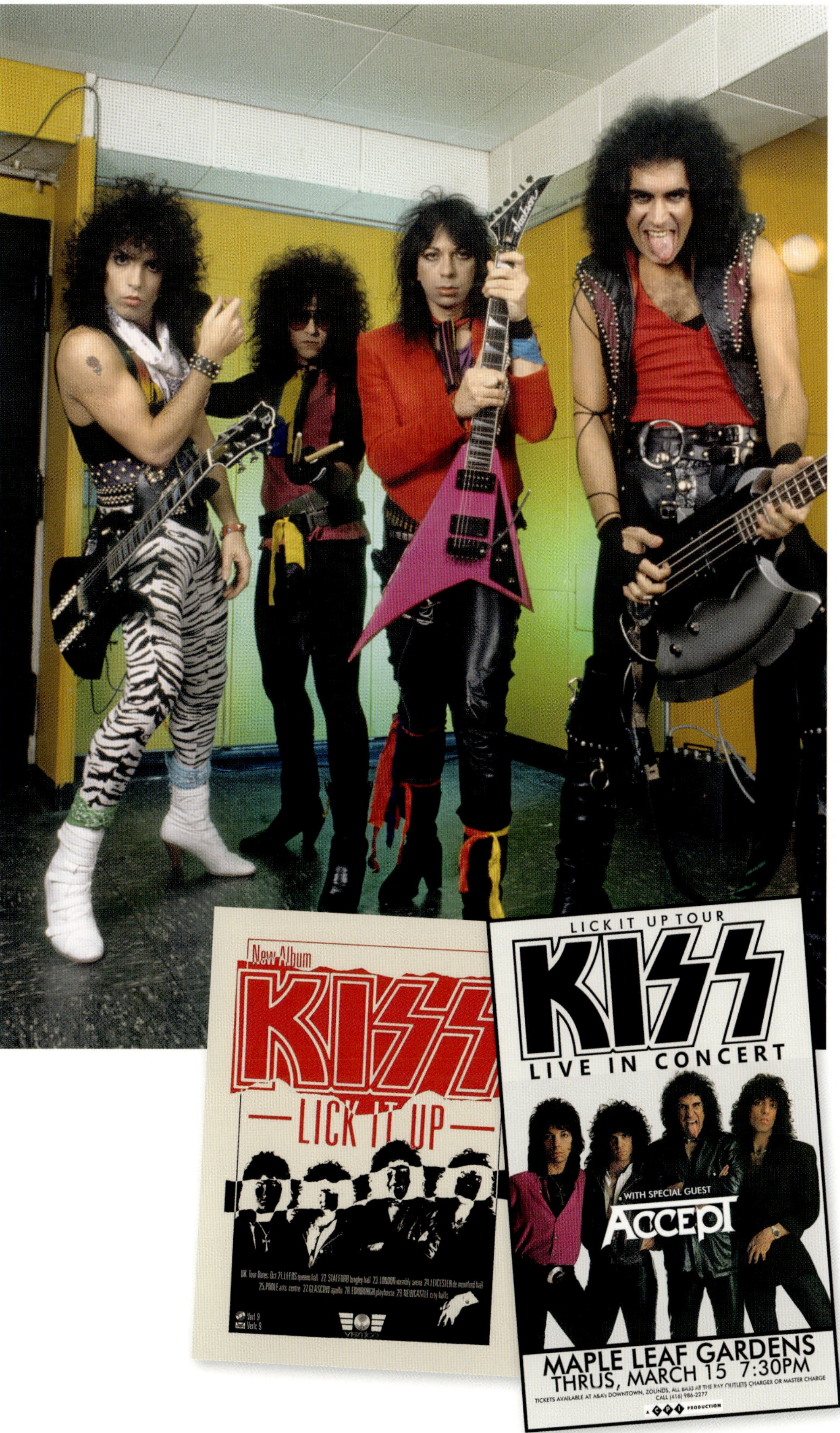

The band poses backstage in their '80s finery, Essen, Germany, November 11, 1983.

There were other issues soon to surface with Vinnie. Eric noticed right away that Vinnie wanted—and expected—everything his way, thinking he could take over the band. Through the making of the album and then into the tour, Vinnie wouldn't sign a contract outlining what and how he was going to get paid, and tensions grew over the fact that the money situation never got locked down. As well, during the shows—the band had repurposed the tank motif from the *Creatures* campaign—Vinnie would hog the spotlight, shredding like a maniac and enraging Paul, who quite clearly was noticing that Vinnie was turning out to be an egomaniac nightmare.

Still, there's no question he helped *Lick It Up* become a spirited and inspired Kiss album, as heavy as *Creatures* but ever so slightly more up-to-date, featuring better writing, more parts and attention to detail, more production, hair metal bravado everywhere—and this was all accomplished with no outside writers.

But a picture is worth a thousand words, or updated, video trumps audio. None of the singles did much on the old-school charts, nor did the album itself light the world on fire, managing a #24 placement at its peak. Indeed, the band's shows, once more, were not that well attended. It was the power of MTV, in conjunction with the band delivering two similar and professional tailor-made videos, that earned *Lick It Up* a gold certification within three months of release, en route to gold status in December 1990, right at the tail end of hair metal's remarkable run of good fortune. But again, it was Kiss (along with, most notably, Aerosmith and Van Halen) that had inspired all these glammy bands effortlessly going platinum in the first place. And now it was Kiss, with *Lick It Up*, that was the first band from a previous generation that was fully committed to this new Hollyrock phenomenon, owning it, leading the way, showing all their old band buddies from 1975 that there was indeed life after death.

Munich, Germany,
November 2, 1983.

KISS
EUROPE 1983
ALL ACCESS
OTTO

27

TURN ON THE NIGHT

ANIMALIZE, FEATURING NEW GUITARIST MARK ST. JOHN

Vinnie dispensed with, Kiss brought to the fold another guitarist without a past, this time not because of makeup issues but because they didn't want another prima donna, not that Vinnie was that way because he was famous. They needed a guy with an appreciation for the job, and that turned out to be Mark St. John, who was also hired because he could play guitar in any number of nonrock styles as well, having served as a guitar teacher as well.

Not that Mark was integral to the new record, *Animalize*, issued on September 13, 1984. To be sure, he played his leads, but he didn't figure in the songwriting, with Paul and Gene splitting the duties, for the most part, with Desmond Child and Mitch Weissman, a songwriter who played Paul in *Beatlemania* and who worked with Gene on songs for Kiss, Keel, and Wendy O. Williams.

But Gene was somewhat inconsequential as well. Having been bitten by the acting bug, he took a few lessons and was working on the Tom Selleck vehicle *Runaway*, which took him away to Hollywood and Vancouver right when the band was finishing up the album, resulting in Paul taking the production credit (Gene is associate producer) as well as handling the mix entirely on his own. Plasmatics bassist Jean Beauvoir cowrites with Paul on "Thrills in the Night," a quality melodic hard rocker with a curiously plodding beat—Beauvoir also deputized for Gene, playing bass on three tracks. Eric gets a single credit, cowriting with Paul and Desmond on "Under the Gun," also providing a noisy double

bass drum barrage on this uncompromising speed metal number. All too predictable, album opener "I've Had Enough (Into the Fire)" was super-heavy as well, although this is a second one held back by a curiously ill-advised beat from Eric.

Elsewhere, "Burn Bitch Burn" reignited the debate about Kiss being male chauvinist pigs, with Gene taking most of the flak, given the fact that he wrote and sang it, delivering the immortal line, "I wanna put my log in your fireplace." The two high points were "Get All You Can Take," which should have been issued as a single, and "Heaven's on Fire," which was. Although this capable follow-up to *Lick It Up* (both feature simple, stacked power chords, gang vocals come chorus time, and convincing exhortations to party) managed only a #49 placement on the charts, once more it was the happy, campy video that mattered, helping push the album platinum within three months of issue, becoming the band's first designation at that level since *Dynasty*. Along with that, the album vaulted to a #19 placement on the charts as part of a thirty-seven-week run. Like "Burn Bitch Burn" and "I've Had

Enough (Into the Fire)," this one had the PMRC and the Moral Majority crowd up in flame-retardant arms as well. The attention didn't hurt—it had been a long time since Kiss were considered hotter than hell, and it felt warm.

As for Paul's production, just like the songs, there was little to discern it from the previous two albums, with Kiss settling into a formula that was working but not breaking any records for sonic dynamism.

What wasn't working was Mark St. John. Already having been deemed frustrating as a studio worker (Paul was annoyed by how hard it was getting suitable solos out of him), once the band hit the road, he developed a case of "reactive arthritis." Truth be told, though, the guys weren't getting along, with Gene's and Paul's East Coast sensibility clashing with Mark's West Coast vibe. After his recovery and then two shows and a partial third, he was officially replaced on December 8, 1984, by his erstwhile stand-in Bruce Kulick, beginning a long period of stability that would serve the band well through to *Carnival of Souls* five albums later.

The "animal" theme is in full effect at Johanneshov Icestadium, Stockholm, Sweden, October 26, 1984.

FROM KISS TO DISCO

LARRY HARRIS ON CASABLANCA

Having passed on in 2017 at the age of seventy, Larry Harris was promotional guru, fix-it man, and all-around second-in-command to Casablanca Records boss Neil Bogart—the two were also second cousins. In the following excerpts from an interview I conducted with him back in 2009, Harris offers insights on why Kiss were such an exciting prospect as the label's first act, and how, in the end, the label wound up more associated with disco.

"The previous company was controlled by a very conservative, educational company called Viewlex," begins Harris, on how Casablanca came to be in the first place. "To be honest with you, my partner and cousin Neil Bogart didn't like being controlled very much. Buddah Records was supposed to have the soundtrack to Woodstock, but Viewlex got in the way. So it was for freedom, really. As for signing Kiss, Kiss was your antihero group. Every kid in America looked at Kiss and went, 'Oh, I can put on makeup and I can hide behind this, and I can say what I want and I can do what I want and my parents hate it, so I'll love it,' which is difficult even today. You know, kids are looking for something to rebel against, something to call their own. Kiss could be called their own, because their parents looked at Kiss and couldn't understand this at all."

Asked about the intended demographic, Harris says, "It was the young male. We didn't know how young when we first went into this, but what sticks out in my mind . . . It was Halloween, probably about 1975 or '76. Neil had younger kids. I didn't have any kids; I wasn't married. So, Neil and I were going out with his kids trick-or-treating. As we walked in the streets of LA, we were seeing kids dressed as Kiss and it blew us away. At that point, we'd never had a band that kids would emulate that way. But that's the thing—they were easy to emulate, just with the makeup and stuff. It was definitely an accident that the demographic was so young. These kids might have seen them on TV or something. But no, it was definitely teenager to twenty-five. But people saw the concerts and told their friends about this great show that they were at. Kiss was able to—because of their stage show, not because of their music—get people really excited about them."

And in the beginning, Casablanca was willing to pull out all the stops to break Kiss.

"Yes, nobody put more money into touring than us," notes Harris. "And we even helped Kiss with their stage show. It was my idea for the drum riser to rise up. Initially, Gene was spitting out fire once, and it was my idea for him to do it more than once. Neil Bogart came up with a bunch of ideas for them. We used to go with them to magic shops to find ideas. We would go into a market and promise the promoter that if he headlined Kiss in the market, if he lost money, we would pay him anything he lost. Nobody had done that at that point. Thank God there were very few markets they lost out in. We overspent on the advertising to the point of it being ridiculous almost. But we felt that the best way for this band to sell albums was for people to see them live. So, we were willing to make that investment. I don't think any label in the world would have spent the kind of money we spent on them."

And yet . . . "We never made a profit," says Harris. "Even with the disco boom, and you know, we had all the big disco acts. We were doing 30, 40 million dollars a year, but we kept putting it back into the business. Plus, we were also pretty well known for the fact that everybody that worked for us flew first class, had limos, a lot of drugs. We were definitely heavy duty into the drug culture."

So even if there was never (officially) a profit, there was certainly a ton of cash flow, especially in the late '70s. This

Gene's proposal to shorten his heels goes nowhere with the Casablanca staff. In all seriousness, label promo man Larry Harris was taken aback by how young Kiss fans skewed.

came from Kiss after the success of *Alive!* and from this new danceable genre of music, sort of two distinct streams, against the usual stable of failing baby bands now lost to history.

"Sure, but product-wise in the end we were just so heavy into disco," affirms Harris. "The label itself wasn't paying so much attention to hard rock because disco was so big at that point. It was its own genre of music. I mean, we still paid attention to our rock bands, but we didn't focus on them marketing-wise as much, because at that point in time, you could do a disco album for about $20,000, whereas a good rock album would cost at least $100,000. You didn't have to tour disco bands because you had all these disco clubs around that made life easy for us. We didn't have to pay for radio airplay as much because the clubs took care of a lot of that. So economically it made more sense—at that point in time—to concentrate on the disco stuff. And a lot of hard rock people started to do disco songs because disco was so popular. I mean, Kiss did one, which pissed off their audience. Cher went from being a rock 'n' roller to having a disco hit, and there were numerous other bands that decided to do a little disco thing here and there.

"It definitely took away some attention," reflects Harris, in closing, "and took away some resources. There was even a station in Chicago that switched to a disco format, which led to the famous disco album burnings. Because that disc jockey—who was fired from the rock station because it went disco—was pissed off and he got a job at another station, and he did this whole thing against disco. But we also had people burning Kiss albums because down in the South they thought they were of the devil and Satan. That was fine with us because they had to buy the albums to burn them. So, burn them all you want—go enjoy yourself."

28

TRIAL BY FIRE

ASYLUM, FEATURING NEW GUITARIST BRUCE KULICK

Whether it's the grainy pastel album cover, the lack of a hit single, or finally an inevitable dose of ageism, come *Asylum*, Kiss found themselves unable to keep up the moderately successful streak they'd put in place over the life cycle of the previous two platters. And it's not because the record, issued on September 16, 1985, and featuring new guitarist Bruce Kulick, wasn't any good. First off, producers Paul and Gene somehow dialed in some nice sounds, creating a sonic picture that is the prettiest—but also the most red-blooded and professional—of all the Kiss albums the band made in the '80s, excepting, arguably, *Elder*.

A rare solo composition from Paul, "Tears Are Falling," was issued as a single, and despite its emotional content and radio-friendly melodies, it failed to capture the imagination of metal fans—of which by this point, it must be said, there were millions and millions. Only they weren't flocking to Kiss anymore, but rather to Dokken, Great White, Ratt, Iron Maiden, Mötley Crüe, and Van Halen. From the old world it was Judas Priest and Scorpions, even if no more than single platinum was the aspiration by the mid-1980s. Cinderella, Poison, Whitesnake, and Guns N' Roses were just around the corner, but truth be told, other baby bands were already on the wane, notably Quiet Riot and Twisted Sister. Soon to ascend was Aerosmith, but that's a freak-of-nature story no one expected. Kiss, on the other hand, found themselves in that blue-collar zone, spending way too much on a show that didn't sell enough tickets to cover the expense, to be sure, delivering but also delivering an illusion.

As for the record, *Asylum* represented a palpable up-ratchet in quality, but again, with timing that was unfortunate. Maybe Kiss were outwearing their welcome, delivering essentially four records in a row coming from the same place, ticking the boxes, including lascivious funk metal Gene songs, lover-man Paul songs, "OTT" (over-the-top) metal—here it's "I'm Alive," "Love's a Deadly Weapon," and to a milder, artier extent, "King of the Mountain"—and then some sort of shot at a single. It must be said that never along the way in the '80s thus far did any of the new lead guitarists do anything remotely enjoyable as music when it comes to guitar solos. Bottom line, we can extol the virtues of Bruce Kulick as a cowriter on three *Asylum* songs and as a team player moving forward, but what he does for leads . . . well, it's of the same frame of mind that Kiss were writing in, namely a sort of ironic and shreddy parody of what it means to be a '70s band fully invested in hair metal.

Nor do I think it really matters that Gene was away doing bit parts in movies and producing Keel and Black 'n Blue albums. Kiss never had a problem yanking in helpers when needed. One guy they didn't use was their own drummer, who had submitted two songs only to have them rejected—Eric would soon resign himself to the fact that he was never going to become a songwriter with the band. None of this mattered, because *Asylum* was as good an album as what came before. Again, it just seemed like people were now familiar with all the tropes of new Kiss, and in conjunction, there were younger bands ploughing the same funky hair metal fields, so why not move on from the old tarts?

In the end, *Asylum* went gold within a couple months of the album's release date, and decisions were made to perpetuate the illusion that the impressive metal-ramped stage show in support of the album meant any semblance of financial sense. Kiss would live to fight another day, and for once it would be without drama at the lead guitar slot. Whether the lack of tension would make for good art is another question, but the point is, Kiss would continue to pack a lunch and go to work.

Kiss's shiny new shredder, Bruce Kulick, at Madison Square Garden, New York City, December 16, 1985.

Madison Square Garden, 1985. Note the over-the-top hair metal costumes. (And, yes, costumes is the right word.)

29
WHILE THE CITY SLEEPS
CRAZY NIGHTS

Producer Ron Nevison's pedigree goes back to Led Zeppelin and Bad Company, through The Babys and UFO. But it was his recent work on bad but super-selling albums with Ozzy Osbourne and Heart that had Paul thinking that hair metal's big producer trope was something worth trying. Nevison indeed expressed his opinions in terms of the songs that would go on the band's fourteenth album, issued on September 21, 1987, and he'd allow keyboards as part of the sweetening process, but he definitely wouldn't get much of a sound for the band. *Crazy Nights* creaks and squeaks like folded cardboard, but then again, maybe with these fully pandering hair metal songs, there's a sort of mainlining effect, or some technological agreement with the compromised fidelity of radio that might have been called for. Not that the label noticed, with staffers at Polygram giving the band a five-minute standing ovation upon hearing the album for the first time.

Who cares what I think, because *Crazy Nights* very quickly went gold, on November 17, and then platinum after a mere five months on the shelves. Now, again, it feels like it was MTV that was responsible rather than the strength of the album. Three plush production videos were produced, accompanying poppy first single "Crazy Crazy Nights," power ballad "Reason to Live," and up-tempo pure hair metal rocker "Turn on the Night." None of the songs did that great as singles, but again, Kiss were all over MTV, with top gun director Marty Callner applying his quick edits and making the band substantively indistinguishable from the bigger fish in the hair pond, namely Whitesnake, Poison, and Bon Jovi.

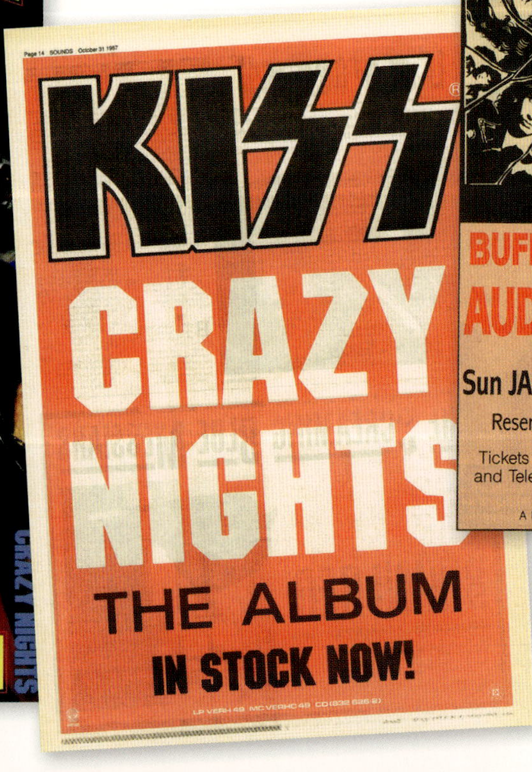

As for who was doing all the work, Nevison indicates that Gene was away for much of the sessions and that most of his time was spent with Paul and Bruce. Eric, as usual, submitted songs and had them rejected. He shows up only on "No No No," an abrasive pile of speed metal noise made all the more screechy by Nevison's horrible production, but in fact ruined by Eric and Bruce before Nevison could botch the mix—"floundering" would be what I'd call it. On the songwriting end, as was the norm during this gratuitously corporate time for Kiss, what we got was either Paul or Gene teamed with a song doctor.

Come tour time it was business as usual. Paul would say that the show was the biggest and most expensive the band had ever mounted and there'd be some truth in that—it was bigger than they could afford. Still, as detailed, the album was a qualified success, again, driven by the release of three Paul-written singles but more important three pop confection videos, one of which accompanied a proper power ballad, which, bafflingly, Kiss hadn't thought about doing since "I Still Love You" from *Creatures of the Night.*

In later years Paul has admitted the record is "a bit plastic-sounding" while Gene calls it "much too pop." Both are true. But if we're to put a positive spin on it, perhaps in retrospect, *Crazy Nights* represents the band keeping with the times, doubling down and incorporating even more hair metal tropes than they had vis-à-vis those known and expected during the nascent years of the movement, say 1983 to 1985. Back to the grousing, this also meant they were doubly oblivious to the fact that a backlash was already in motion, and that come the rise of Soundgarden, Nirvana, Alice in Chains, and Pearl Jam, what they were doing on a record like this would very soon be seen as laughable.

The band makes a rare club appearance at **The Ritz** in New York City, August 12, 1988.

30

FIREHOUSE
HOT IN THE SHADE

One little discussed benefit of being a heritage act with a lot of success is the greatest hits album, which often flies under the radar when discussing a band's numbers but is often the best-selling album of a catalog. Kiss went into the *Hot in the Shade* album cycle not only with *Crazy Nights* having already gone platinum, but with an interim compilation called *Smashes, Thrashes & Hits* also having seen platinum en route to double platinum status in 1996. For the record, the band remixed a bunch of songs, wrote two naughty new tracks, and had "Beth" redone with Eric singing it.

And although Eric got but one cowriting credit across fifteen tracks totaling an hour on *Hot in the Shade*, he gets a lead vocal, demonstrating on "Little Caesar" that he has every bit as good a vocal technique as Gene and Paul with a God-given good voice as well—one wonders if the band might have missed out on a clutch of hit singles given Carr's high and soulful and radio-friendly voice.

Elsewhere it's business as usual, with one small adjustment: Gene and Paul are back as producers with the idea of making a bit more of a raw and rocking album, working at a down-market studio called The Fortress and indeed using demo versions of some of the songs as basic tracks. But despite noisy rock barrages like "Betrayed," "Cadillac Dreams," and the ridiculous "Boomerang," the guys take care of business, offering as a first single pop rocker "Hide Your Heart" and coughing up another rulebook power ballad in "Forever," which found Paul cowriting with Michael Bolton. Both got corporate hair metal videos, as did swaggering opening track "Rise to It."

Also according to formula, the writing of the songs was split between Paul and Gene, each working with an outside assembly-line song doctor, including Vini Poncia, who returns to the fold showing up five times. Bruce (yes, a member of the band) is there twice, as is Black 'n Blue axeman Tommy Thayer, who one day would replace Kulick (or technically Ace, if he was ever seriously part of Kiss the second time).

And why fifteen songs? Well, late 1989 was when the United States made the switch from vinyl LP to compact disc, and it's admirable that Kiss were there immediately offering value for the money. Of course, the vinyl was also still widely produced and distributed, but cramming a half hour of material onto each side made for a thin and screechy listening experience, aggravated by the fact that Paul and Gene had already produced the album to their characteristically dry, boxy standards.

It was the success of #8-charting "Forever" as a single, released on January 5, 1990, that gave *Hot in the Shade* legs and helped put bums in the seats on the ensuing tour, where the band played in front of an elaborate Sphinx-themed stage. The album had already gone gold by this point, having achieved that status on December 20, 1989, along with a #29 placement on the Billboard charts. Also key was the presence of three glossy videos stacked high with hair clichés, keeping Kiss in front of MTV's sugar-rushed viewership. The fact that the album didn't reach platinum perhaps served as a canary in the coalmine that the party up and down the Sunset Strip was about to end. The formula had gotten predictable and tired. How tired? After Bonnie Tyler had already recorded it the previous year, "Hide Your Heart"—granted, written by Paul, Desmond Child, and Holly Knight—was recorded four times in 1989, by Molly Hatchet, Robin Beck, Kiss, and . . . Ace Frehley.

On the eve of hair metal's demise, Long Beach Arena, Long Beach, California, September 14, 1990.

Supporting *Hot in the Shade* at Long Beach Arena, September 14, 1990.

31

COMIN' HOME

LONGTIME KISS DRUMMER ERIC CARR SUCCUMBS TO CANCER

According to his sister, Eric had been sick with the cancer that would kill him as far back as the *Hot in the Shade* tour. What was to be his last concert turned out to be a hometown stand at Madison Square Garden, November 9, 1990, with his last song performed being a typically spirited hustle through "Rock and Roll All Nite."

By February 1991 he had been coughing up blood and feeling ill with a rare diagnosis of heart cancer, resulting in open heart surgery in April to remove the tumor—it's all there on YouTube for the world to see, with Eric giving the post-operation play-by-play on April 12. The night before the operation, Gene and Paul had visited him in the hospital and got McDonald's for Eric. They returned a few days later to check up on him and he was in good spirits. He did not tell the guys it was cancer.

Being cooped up in the hospital was additionally anxious for Eric because Kiss were gearing up to record a new album. As a preliminary move, Gene and Paul had retested their relationship with Bob Ezrin by working with him on the song "God Gave Rock 'n' Roll to You II," which was slated for the *Bill & Ted's Bogus Journey* soundtrack album. The drummer on the song is Eric Singer, who had recently played in Paul's low-key solo band. Eric Carr, in a sense wanting to continue to work but also guarding his turf, insisted on flying to California in July 1991 to be in the music video for the song, which he accomplished (wearing a wig, given that he had lost all his hair), working until three in the morning and then flying right back to New York

afterward and reentering the hospital. In the lead-up to Eric's death he had suffered an aneurysm and then a brain hemorrhage and went into a coma. He died on November 24, 1991, the same day we lost Freddie Mercury, the news of which dominated the headlines.

The band attended the funeral, which was held on November 30 in a Catholic church in Middletown, New York, where his parents had moved from Brooklyn. Ace was there as well, but he sat in a different part of the church. At the last minute, the service was opened up to fans as well. Bruce cried and Paul cried but Gene was seen just staring straight ahead in disbelief, forgetting to stand when the attendees were instructed to. The procession to the burial site at the Cedar Hill Cemetery in nearby Newburgh was 2 miles (3.6 km) long, with the fan contingent not allowed into the mausoleum. After it was over, they were allowed into the cemetery grounds and paid their respects a second time.

Kiss's next album, *Revenge*, would be dedicated to Eric and would include a drum showcase track called "Carr Jam 1981," recorded during the *Music from the Elder* sessions, with Ace swapped out for Bruce. Also of note, in 1999 there was a posthumous Eric Carr solo album called *Rockology*, which once again makes it all too clear that Eric was an absolutely top-shelf lead singer, making his passing at the age of forty-one all the more poignant.

Eric Carr at Radio City
Music Hall, New York,
March 10, 1984.

32

BANG BANG YOU

REVENGE, FEATURING NEW DRUMMER ERIC SINGER

A plethora of things lined up to make *Revenge* the best Kiss album of the Bruce Kulick era, one being that the second-banana guitarist really came into his own as a maker of music come solo time. Then there's his cowrite on "Tough Love," one of the best songs of a fine batch, arguably blessed with the record's most sophisticated an' scientific riff. No doubt an element to the ascendance of Kulick would be the fact that Bob Ezrin was back producing the band. Ezrin was known for demanding dedication and effort from his players, and he would have spotted what he liked from Kulick and what needed to be discarded, doing much the same with new drummer Eric Singer and to a lesser, more deferential extent, Gene and Paul.

But that's what Gene and Paul liked about Ezrin back in the *Destroyer* days, that he wanted hard work and attention to detail, and there's no question that the performances, arrangements—even the sheer number of parts across *Revenge* and what happens at the end of each bar—reflect craft, elbow grease, really wanting it. What we don't get is the conceptual Ezrin from *The Elder* or *The Wall* or even "Great Expectations." Instead, it's the taskmaster but also the guy who gets into the guts of the songs, which is reflected in the fact that he's credited six times as a cowriter. Final point, Ezrin has never been noted for consistently making high-fidelity records, but he nails it with *Revenge*, placing everything smartly and boldly in the mix, providing ample bottom end, resulting in the best-sounding record the band ever made, both backward and forward.

Another intriguing narrative is the fact that Vinnie Vincent resurfaced, swearing up and down that he'd changed, asking if he could write some songs. Surprisingly, Gene gave him a chance, and we got pounding opener "Unholy," heralded as the return of Gene as the demon (literally), an image reinforced by his new unshaven, glaring rough an' tumble look. Vinnie also collaborated with Paul on the middling "Heart of Chrome" and the joyous "I Just Wanna." Unfortunately, as Gene frames it, Vinnie soon wanted to renegotiate his arrangement with the guys and quickly and unceremoniously was sent packing (after leaving the songs on the table).

The resulting record, issued on May 19, 1992, turned out to be an embarrassment of riches, with the likes of "Take It Off," "Spit," "Thou Shalt Not," and "Domino" all worthy as rockin' singles. Of those, only "Domino" was tried, as was "Unholy," "I Just Wanna," and ballad "Every Time I Look at You," on which Ezrin gets to do his strings thing while Bruce plays acoustic. Already a single months ago but part of the album

Introducing the new guy, Eric Singer (lower left) in Munich, Germany, June 2, 1992.

and making it even stronger was "God Gave Rock 'n' Roll to You II." It's the only song that made much of a dent in the public consciousness, but this time we can blame the lack of excitement on huge cultural shifts in the type of hard rock that was popular. Pearl Jam's *Ten* had come out in August 1991, followed by Nirvana's *Nevermind* in September, and grunge was all the rage. What Kiss were left with was the most professional album they'd ever done, but it was built inside an idiom of the past.

In fact, industry watchers at this point were impressed that *Revenge* even managed gold given the horror stories starting to pile up of utter bombs by bands that were titans just a few years earlier—and that's from the ones that still had their major label deals. That might be a bit of an exaggeration, as it definitely got worse in 1993, and the next year and the next. But still, on everyone's lips was the idea that it was over for hair metal, and indeed when anybody talked about Kiss in the press in 1992, it was to say how stupid it was to write songs about strippers.

Still, the record managed a #6 placement on Billboard, and like much of the recent catalog, it did well in Canada and overseas. But none of these minor victories, nor the floating of fully five singles for fan consideration, could nudge the album up into the platinum status they'd managed with the vastly inferior (but better timed) *Crazy Nights* album just five years earlier. If there was ever a time for the famously cynical Gene to be cynical about the music business, that would be now. He'd delivered a masterpiece, possibly the culmination of everything Kiss were about crafted to diamond-hard perfection, and yet out in the world, beyond those who'd already stuck the fork in, *Revenge* had been met with little more than polite applause. In other words, a great Kiss record, but the bar isn't very high, is it?

33

SHOUT IT OUT LOUD

ALIVE III

Kiss are known to be smart with their business, so the mind boggles why there was no *Alive III* after the *Creatures of the Night*, *Lick It Up*, and *Animalize* trilogy (let's ignore the previous trio). Many bands had successful double live albums at that time, and a gatefolded, picture-stuffed offering from Kiss would have gone platinum easily, especially with the ol' double counting for double albums.

In any event, here it comes, on May 18, 1993, and like *Revenge* going gold, it's even more surprising that *Alive III* finds gold (and a #9 placement on Billboard), as we're now deep into the death of Hollyrock. Mind you, it took eighteen months, but let's not forget that this was a single long CD and therefore not double-counted like *Alive!* and *Alive II*.

Across an action-packed track list that demonstrates how many great songs the band wrote in the '80s, *Alive III* executes a one-song overlap with *Alive II* ("Detroit Rock City"), but includes three from *Alive!*, namely "Watchin' You," "Rock and Roll All Nite," and an insanely pounding "Deuce." From the wilderness years, only "I Was Made for Loving You" emerges, and for this the guys had to perform and record it at a sound check, after which crowd noise was added (opening the door for suspicion about further doctoring). Another wrinkle is the inclusion of three power ballads—"Forever," "I Still Love You," and "God Gave Rock 'n' Roll to You II"—with the latter fuzzy-feeling song put in the penultimate position before Brice wangs off on a pyro-strafed "Star-Spangled Banner."

As for the rest, it's a rock 'n' roll party in the streets, with the band on fire, slamming their way through two more from *Creatures of the Night*, one each from *Lick It Up* and *Animalize*, nothing from the next three other than "Forever," and then three more from *Revenge* ("Take It Off" was added as an international bonus track).

Back "producing" is Eddie Kramer, magician at the helm for the previous two live albums, with the band recording shows in late November 1992 in Detroit, Indianapolis, and Cleveland. As for packaging, amid a couple of errors in the liner notes about what songs come from what albums, graciously, the entire crew gets name-checked in big type and by job description—nestled halfway through we see the name of hidden performing keyboardist Derek Sherinian, of Dream Theater fame. There's also a pretty serious Kiss family tree that includes entries for the likes of Treasure, Good Rats, Blackjack, White Tiger, and Badlands. Of note, we see Eric Singer's rise up the food chain from Lita Ford through Black Sabbath, Gary Moore, Badlands, and Alice Cooper.

As a nice throwback to *Alive!* there's a signed note from the guys that reads, "When we're dead and gone, how are we remembered?? Only by what we leave behind. If talk is cheap, action is worth its weight in gold and platinum! *Alive I* (*sic*), *II*, and now *Alive III* will be our testament, our monument to us, to you, and to the invincibility of Rock + Roll."

Anticipating the release of *Alive III*, somewhere in So-Cal, 1993.

PART FOUR
REUNION

The reunion is on!
Everything old is new
again, 1996.

34

GET ALL YOU CAN TAKE

THE FIRST OFFICIAL WORLDWIDE KISS CONVENTION

Fully surreal, the kickoff event for the official Kiss conventions of 1995 saw Gene and Paul and a bunch of cops raid a typical fan-mounted convention in Troy, Michigan, on July 17, 1994. With the shopping locals losing their minds, expressing confusion mixed with giddy fandom, the guys walked through the place pointing out and grabbing costumes and boots, officially seizing them, claiming that they were ill-gotten. As Paul explained, it had to be done by surprise—any announcement, and the booty would have been whisked away. It's a long story—and no one knows for sure the nuances of the tale—but it seems that Bill Aucoin, no longer managing the band and not wanting to continue paying storage fees, had auctioned off the contents of a storage locker full of Kiss kit, apparently offering it first to Kiss management, who had said no. The question hung in the air: Who actually owned this stuff and was legally entitled to sell it? Even if the purchasers paid good cash for it in good faith, were they buying high-heeled shoes that were hot or at least warm?

In any event, Kiss smartly and successfully took back these fashion accessories from their past, some say partly because they had already hatched a plan to mount their own rock 'n' rolling Kiss museum, which is what these glorified Kiss-themed record shows had become.

The band tested the concept on the Australian tour in February 1995, following a string of Japanese dates the previous month. Amusingly, illustrated by the behavior of the good people from Perth at the local Hyatt on February 3, they decided alcohol should not be served at these things. Once transported over to America, a full-blown convention tour ensued, beginning at the Burbank Airport Hilton & Convention Center in California on June 17. And credit to the band, they did it up right. Justifying the $100 ticket, a typical convention was a noon-to-midnight affair. Included were Q&As, tribute bands, clinics with Eric and Bruce, autograph sessions, a major Kiss museum, and vendors everywhere. Fans got to see original cover artworks, handwritten lyrics, and guitars and drum sets used live and in the studio. The highlight was an extensive acoustic set, where the band played with no props or special lights, bringing out many deep tracks at the request of fans. On opening night, they were joined by Peter Criss, who sang "Hard Luck Woman" and "Nothin' to Lose."

Kiss hold a press conference and live performance at the Hard Rock Café in Los Angeles, June 16, 1995. The event was a kickoff to the Kiss Convention Tour 1995–1996.

Kiss Convention attendee Greg Omodt of Brookings, South Dakota, enjoys an acoustic performance by the band.

As Gene put it, Kiss were knocking down the wall (or crossing the moat) that had always been there between the band and the fans, and credit where credit is due, this was a fresh entrepreneurial venture offering good value. Also deserving credit is Tommy Thayer, who ably managed the tour, proving himself beyond his skills as guitarist in Black 'n Blue. Really, one's character comes out more in the thousands of little decisions that have to happen "tour managing," especially something novel like this, which involved curating as well. Soon he'd be the long-standing guitarist in Kiss and you just know that his trial by fire was more so this kind of grinding work and less so the occasional cowrite or backing vocal or how well he strummed.

All told, even though the entrance fee for the convention seemed steep at the time, over the years access to the band would become much more restricted and much more expensive. In that light, the convention tour seems like the last vestige of an ideal and naive—and pre-Internet—time before the collecting of records and rock memorabilia was to go on a rocket ride in both popularity and price. Bottom line: No Kiss fan is complaining anymore about the lifetime of memories they got for a hundred bucks back in 1995.

35

ANY WAY YOU WANT IT

KISS PERFORM ON *MTV UNPLUGGED*

As things go in the film industry, it takes a fan on the inside (plus some luck) to get a project from dumb idea to good idea to fruition, and at MTV, that guy was Alex Coletti. As for the luck, that was the confluence of events that saw Kiss exercising over and over again the acoustic rendition muscle through their performances at the Kiss conventions. Tying it together, Coletti had attended the Detroit stop on July 22, 1995, and saw how good the band was and how effusively the crowd responded, as if that could have gone any other way.

Paul and Gene quickly invited Peter and Ace. The Catman turned out to be easy—the LA opening where Peter cameoed went free an' easy, no hassles. Ace, on the other hand, made all sorts of demands, including $5,000, some roadies, and hotel suites for both himself and his daughter Monique. Once the guys got down to rehearsals, they were surprised at how difficult the task was proving. There was the challenge to go that extra step toward what MTV expected in terms of "unplugged," plus "Beth" was a challenge, as was getting Peter up to snuff on the drumming end. Helping, however, was the fact that Peter and Ace had actually just finished a club tour together as The Bad Boys of Kiss.

Four days of rehearsals at SIR in New York, with an MTV crew present, led to a four-hour proper filming session at Sony on August 9, 1995. Numerous takes were needed of most of the songs, partly because MTV wanted to find the best bits and quips between songs—not like they succeeded, with some of it coming off as awkward, especially when Ace opens his mouth.

Without knowing how much practice and editing went into the project, the performance comes off as effortless, as if we're watching seasoned pros proving that at the heart of what they do, they are old-school entertainers with sturdy songs that can be played around a campfire. Of course, the set list was carefully curated to work this way, and the band had already done much of that heavy lifting by trying so many different fan requests during the conventions, along with playing more than would be needed in rehearsals and even at the filmed final session.

The show appeared on MTV on October 31, 1995, with the CD to follow on March 12, 1996, after protracted negotiations between MTV and Mercury. The songs performed and recorded are mostly fresh, unexpected choices. "Plaster Caster" and "Domino" were fully oddball. Given the mandate, there are a number of ballads, including "Goin' Blind," "Sure Know Something," "A World Without Heroes," "I Still Love You," "Every Time I Look at You," "Beth," and the obscure Gene Simmons solo album song "See You Tonight," which proves to be a magic Beatles-esque moment on the album. But "Comin' Home," "Nothin' to Lose," and "2000 Man" are full-on Rolling Stones, with the actual Stones cover serving as somewhat of a highlight, given Ace's holler-along vocal. "Nothin' to Lose" is fun as well because the vocal is a duet between Peter and Eric, who sings a lead vocal for the first time on a Kiss album—like Eric Carr before him, he's really good. All four of the originals sing on album closer (and single) "Rock and Roll All Nite," with Gene proving his vocal chops as he and Paul both do across the expanse of this beautifully executed and recorded album.

MTV Unplugged was certified gold on May 15, 1996, reaching #15 on the Billboard charts and also doing well internationally. As far as Kiss fans were concerned, it served as proof that the originals could and would be getting back together, something Eric had been sensibly worried about during the process. There had even been an uncomfortable bit of booing when Bruce and Eric came back onstage for the final number, with Ace finding it necessary to say, "C'mon, man, these guys are part of the family too."

The Starman and one of his distinctive Washburn signature guitars during the band's two-day stand at the Fleet Center in Boston, Massachusetts, July 30 and 31, 1996.

36

UNHOLY

CARNIVAL OF SOULS: THE FINAL SESSIONS

"It ain't that dark in Beverly Hills," quipped Paul, expressing reservations about making a doomy grunge album. Gene, on the other hand, was all-in, having both the growling voice and the hairy look of a Bigfoot harboring dark thoughts in the rain forests of the Pacific Northwest. In any event, the band entered Music Grinder Studios in Hollywood in February 1996, working with Slayer and Alice in Chains producer Toby Wright on eleven songs that were supposed to come out on an album called *Head*.

Instead, a deal had been struck for the original band to mount a reunion tour, in makeup, and the album was shelved, only to be leaked in bootleg form. It emerged officially almost two years later, on October 28, 1997, with an acceptable title but an undercutting subtitle, *The Final Sessions*. Also delegitimizing *Carnival of Souls* was the cover art, which showed the band bored in a jam room, the photograph distorted and washed out. For a booklet, we got four panels comprising two pictures of the band and sparse credits, top to bottom designed poorly.

There'd also be no tour, no interviews, and no video, although geometric Soundgarden tribute "Jungle" was issued as a single. One of the lighter numbers—and even those are written in the heroin chic grunge idiom—like "Childhood's End" or "I Will Be There" or "Seduction of the Innocent" might have stood a fighting change, but truth be told, a bunch of old fart bands had tried alternative metal by this point and they weren't fooling anyone. "I Will Be There" was inspired by the birth of Paul's son Evan, with Paul commenting that it's the only song he felt connected to on the entire album. This one does the Led Zeppelin *III* thing grunge bands liked, whereas something like "Seduction of the Innocent" does the psychedelic Beatles "Norwegian Wood" thing grunge bands did, also explored by Warrant, Dokken, Skid Row, Def Leppard, and Ozzy Osbourne, with only Ozzy getting away with it, but just barely.

As Bruce amusingly points out, he's heard fans call *Carnival of Souls* the best Kiss album ever and the worst Kiss album ever. It certainly commits completely to heavy grunge, wallowing in atmospherics and then perked up by circular riffs atop odd time signatures. Eric seems to be having fun (even if he gets no writing credits), and "I Walk Alone" finds Bruce providing a lead vocal, albeit on the last track of this opaque one-hour-long album.

Given the rousing success that was the reunion tour, both Eric and Bruce might have thought their days with Kiss were over. That was indeed to be the case with Bruce, but Eric would soon be back drumming with the band, albeit in Peter's makeup. *Carnival of Souls* therefore turned out to be the last of the Bruce Kulick era but also the last of the nonmakeup era, serving also as the one and only time the band fancied a run at Alice in Chains.

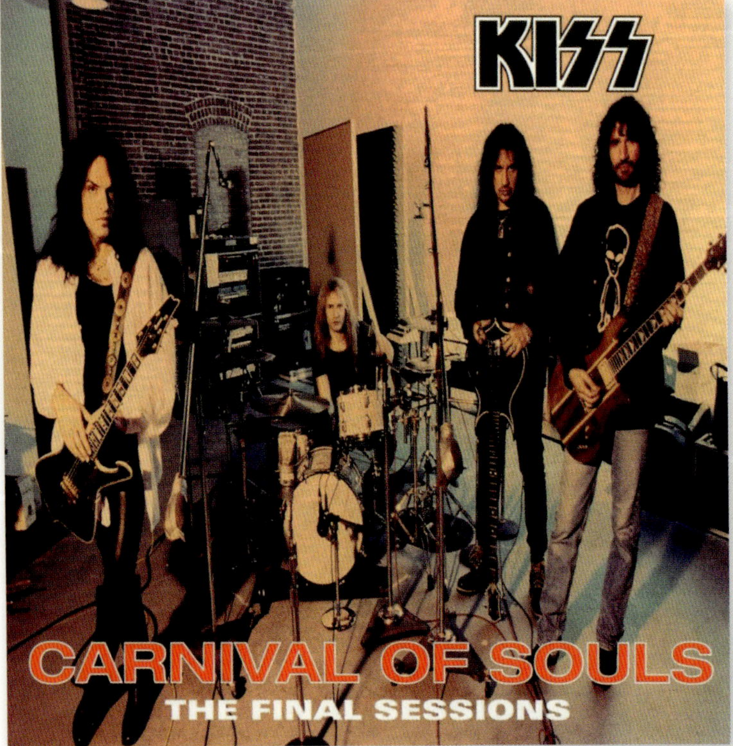

Peter Criss, back in business but throwing a wrench into plans to promote *Carnival of Souls*, Finsbury Park, London, July 5, 1997.

37

I STILL LOVE YOU

CLASSIC-ERA KISS LINEUP ISSUES PSYCHO CIRCUS

Having spent the latter half of 1996 and all of 1997 back on top, taking the big reunion show around the world, including Japan, Australia, South America, and Europe, the classic Kiss lineup had one more piece of business to take care of, and that's making a record. Unfortunately, relations between Gene and Paul on one side and Peter and Ace on the other had deteriorated over the pressure cooker of touring duties. Ace would show up late for work, sometimes high, sometimes drunk, and not put the hours in on his fitness training. And both of them, according to Gene, suffered from memory loss and were often paranoid and complaining about money, despite having their terms of employment laid out very clearly in their contracts.

So the resulting much-vaunted reunion album, *Psycho Circus,* issued on September 22, 1998, was classic lineup in name only. Ace would play guitar and provide lead vocals on the one song he wrote, "Into the Void," and participate on the rousing all-hands-on-deck "You Wanted the Best." Peter would sing on the horrible ballad "I Finally Found My Way" and "You Wanted the Best" and drum on one song only: Ace's "Into the Void." Donnie Iris and the Cruisers drummer Kevin Valentine, who last helped out on *Hot in the Shade* and *Revenge,* would pound the skins on the album's nine other songs, while Tommy Thayer would provide most of the lead guitar, with Bruce Kulick also helping out.

As Ace told me, "Paul and Gene were fighting over the songs we were going to get on the record (laughs). There's so much competition. I mean, that was one of the things that wasn't so fun about Kiss. There was a lot of rivalry. Not really negative rivalry, but everybody always wanted the spotlight. You've got four lead singers in the band, and everybody was like 'Me, me, me, me.' Not so much me—well, maybe (laughs). But a lot of times I was content to just play guitar. In fact, a couple of the songs that I'm doing now were actually submitted for *Psycho Circus.* 'Pursuit of Rock 'n' Roll,' that's one, and I'm not sure if I submitted 'Hard for Me' or 'Steamroller.'"

Producing the sessions at A&M in Hollywood, with the mix happening at One on One in New York, would be Vancouver legend Bruce Fairbairn (Loverboy, Bon Jovi, Aerosmith), to no discernible positive effect. Fairbairn would die a year later, while working on *The Ladder* for prog rockers Yes. The album had actually been started with Bob Ezrin, but Gene and Paul figured his eye wasn't on the ball, being busy at the time with Internet ventures. In fairness to Fairbairn, Gene had told him at a meeting in Winnipeg that the job would be "torture," and that's how it turned out, with most of the grief coming from Ace and Peter.

With only ten tracks, *Psycho Circus* leaves nowhere to hide. Still, there are some worthy songs as part of this small batch. The opening title track is anthemic enough, with Kiss embracing simplicity like the days of yore, pushing big hanging chords here and there, beneath lyrics that literally include "Welcome to the show" on a song that is

written to be a show opener. "I Pledge Allegiance to the State of Rock & Roll" is even stronger, mixing a melodic verse structure with a building prechorus and finally a chorus that is the best of the brew. Ace's song is typically hard-hitting, and then "You Wanted the Best" is another roustabout rocker built for the stage. Elsewhere, "Within" is a downer and ill-placed as the second song on the album. "We Are One" is maudlin, as is Peter's ballad, but closer "Journey of 1,000 Years," written and sung by Gene, is lighter Kiss done well, even thoughtfully. There's a bit of prog-minded old Alice Cooper to this one, with "Raise Your Glasses" also evoking Alice, but more so his hair metal era around *Trash* and *Hey Stoopid*, when, really, he and Kiss were doing much the same thing.

With all the heavy touring just past and to come, as well as with the pictures of Gene, Paul, Ace, and Peter on the back of the swell cover art, it's no surprise that *Psycho Circus* certified gold and reached a lofty #3 on the Billboard charts. As had become the norm for Kiss, there were strong sales around the world, with the band's hottest territory away, Australia, sending the record to #1.

Down the years, Paul became dismissive of *Psycho Circus*. "I thought parts of it were really great," he told me in 2005. "And I also thought that there was some material that didn't measure up. And I also thought that there was a producer who didn't really have a clue about what the band was. And you know, as I came to realize that this may be somebody's first Kiss album, it's not mine. And that's enough reason to not have to explain myself too often."

A return to the classic-era lineup also meant a return to classic-looking stage wear. Madison Square Garden, New York City, November 23, 1998.

It was always a pleasure to chat with classic-era Kiss manager Bill Aucoin, and now that he's no longer with us— he passed on in 2010 at the age of sixty-six—I wanted to take the opportunity to "put in the history books" some of his thoughts on what he had accomplished with the guys, including a few memories of the vintage days as well as where he sat with the boys from the vantage point of the early 2000s, which is indeed where we begin . . .

"Just off and on," reflects Aucoin, asked about whether he stays in touch with Paul and Gene. "Every once in a while I'll get a call from Gene or I'll see Ace or Peter. I made it a point when they all split up that I would make sure and go on the road and see them. Ace I've seen a few times on the road, same with Peter, and of course at some of the Kiss conventions. It's funny; it's almost like a marriage, something you can't really go back to. You know, we talked a bit about all of us getting back together again on this latest reunion. But to do it other than just for the money, it would never be the same as just going through the beginnings of it. It's just a business and it's not creative from the point of view of what I have lived through, and that's what I love, so . . ."

Asked about what caused the break in relations back in 1982, Aucoin says, "For me, it was because things were changing. I didn't want Peter to leave. I thought if anything, we should help him through any problems he was having. Same thing with Ace, although that happened after I left. But I knew it was happening. I really thought the development of Kiss was an entity that had a life of its own. It wasn't just Gene or Paul or Peter or Ace— it was Kiss. And in the midst of all of that, the group really didn't want to be together, and they certainly didn't want to do albums. I mean, *The Elder* was a Bob Ezrin album; it wasn't a Kiss album. And the only reason it got done is that Bob said he would deliver an album. They didn't want to be in the studio together, and they didn't really want to record, to be honest with you. And then of course that turned out to be a horror story.

"On top of that they wanted to take off their makeup," Aucoin continues. "I think Gene and Paul finally wanted to be known. I think they were a little taken aback by the fact they weren't known like other superstars. And on top of that, they wanted to stop the merchandising. They thought it was getting too kiddie-ish and getting younger and younger. And I said, 'Look, you've built something here that is too important. You can't just say no to all of this. You can't just turn it off.' But they decided that was the case. So we were in conflict on a number of things, and I think it was better that we split. I found it ironic that over the years, after we had split, they started doing everything exactly the way I had wanted it years before. To the point where they got it all back together again and did everything we did and more, including pushing the envelope in merchandising over the last few years. So what can I say (laughs)?

"Determined," says Aucoin with a laugh, asked to describe the guys in terms of their psychology. "Not at all what you would think. Certainly not the persona. Paul is more the persona than Gene, who is less of a rock 'n' roller. Paul, I think, was a rock 'n' roller, but not as much as Peter and Ace. Peter and Ace just lived and loved it. Paul has really turned out wonderfully. He's really got command of the stage. I was thrilled for him doing *Phantom of the Opera*. In the back of my mind and heart I really think that Paul might come out of this being the real star. Because he's capable, he's hardworking, he's learned his lessons. He's really learned his lessons as it applies to the stage, and I think it really shows when he did *Phantom of the Opera* up in Canada. There is just no question that Paul has stamina. I think he may turn out to be the real star of all of this as time goes on.

NBC News correspondent Edwin Newman (third from left), on-camera reporter for *NBC Reports*, with Bill Aucoin and the band, December 16, 1977.

"Also, the great thing about Paul is that he cares so much. He really does, and that I think will do him well. Whereas Gene—I'll give you a great example: When Gene had his record label on RCA, Simmons Records, Gene would sometimes get monitor mixes from the groups that he was signing, and if he thought they were halfway decent, instead of ever having to mix the album, he'd put out the monitor mixes and save the money for himself (laughs). It's not that Gene doesn't know. You can't do twenty-five albums and not know what you're doing. The question is whether or not he's going to take the time to make it into something really special that can sell millions of records or whether it's going to be, 'Okay, this is it, next.'

"Now Peter, he certainly did have those influences in him that he claims, all those jazz influences," continues Aucoin, asked if we were only seeing the tip of the iceberg with Peter Criss as far as his skills went. "But the great thing about Peter is his love for rock 'n' roll, which goes beyond anything. I don't think there is anything beyond rock 'n' roll in his life. If it wasn't for Peter and Ace, there wouldn't be a lot of rock 'n' roll influence in Kiss. The fact that Peter might now be slowing down a bit, and everything is pretty much straight ahead and maybe not quite as exciting, you know, at least he's there. And half the battle is just being there."

And it was always a battle, says Aucoin. "Yes, well, to start with (Casablanca head) Neil (Bogart) was a crazy person, but a great guy. The great thing about Neil was that we could come up with an idea and we could sit over a desk or table or a drink and if you shook your hand on it, you knew you didn't need paperwork. We always did paperwork, but he was that kind of guy. 'We're going to do this?!' 'Yes.' And that was it. You knew it was going to be done no matter how crazy.

"One of my philosophies is that you never try to do anything mediocre. Let people love you or hate you, but never get caught in the middle. The other thing is, if you're going to do something, you just have to decide to do it all the way. You are lucky if people don't really want to be on your side. I find that if everybody thinks it's a hit and everybody thinks it's going to be successful, everybody drains you. They all want to be around. Everybody wants to be part of it, and that kind of drains the energy from the idea. If in fact people are a little scared of it, you can do almost anything because then your energy isn't depleted. And we were lucky because radio hated us—most people hated us—so we really did what we wanted. People really did not want to get near us. They assumed that we were just going to die sooner or later and they didn't want to be part of this death knell (laughs). So we did most of what we wanted without too much adversity from the inside. We had all the adversity you could want from the outside."

38

OUTTA THIS WORLD

KISS PERFORM AT SUPER BOWL XXXIII

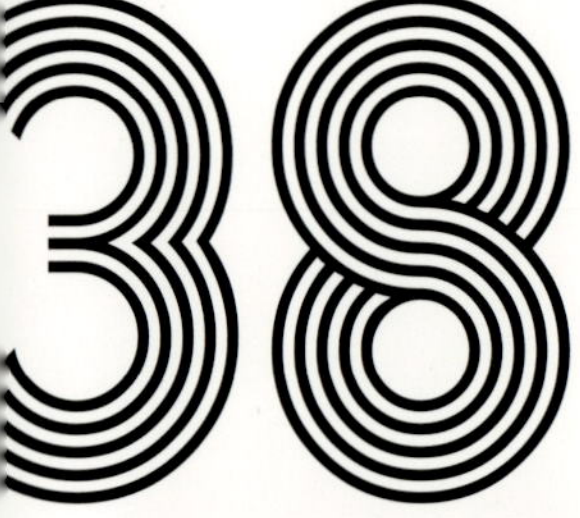

Perhaps the true career highlight or milestone of the reunion period is the enormous amount of touring the band managed, rather than *MTV Unplugged* or *Psycho Circus* or what we are celebrating here: the day Kiss played the Super Bowl. But still, despite all those huge shows, it's pretty cool to play for a massive mainstream crowd on national TV in prime time. Kiss had been here before, and they knew the promotional value of such opportunities, especially when they had a new album to promote.

The occasion was the 33rd annual National Football League showdown, taking place at Pro Player Stadium in Miami on January 31, 1999. Kiss wasn't playing at halftime—that was something called "A Celebration of Soul, Salsa, and Swing" featuring Big Bad Voodoo Daddy, Stevie Wonder, and Gloria Estefan—but rather they were the pregame entertainment, followed by former Gene Simmons paramour Cher singing the national anthem.

The band was set up in an end zone on a fairly sparse stage. But once the relentless pyro barrage started, it looked like a typical larger-than-life Kiss show. Gene was fully resplendent in his bulkiest, most elaborate demon costume as he capably hollered out the band's lone selection, "Rock and Roll All Nite." Paul was bare-chested, Peter looked a little wild, and the band's most unpredictable and crazy member, Ace, looked typically cleanest as Spaceman.

When Ace went to do his guitar solo, sparklers twirled around at the end of his headstock. The field in front of the band was filled with dancing cheerleaders in full makeup, and huge flags were rolled out representing the two teams (Denver and Atlanta) about to do battle. Halfway through, huge black risers went up with Gene on one of them and Ace on the other. At the end of the song, amid all manner of flames and smoke, Paul did one of his traditional guitar smashings.

If we are to look for one additional way to make this a Kiss career milestone, it is the fact that Kiss became the first true hard rock band to do something like this. To be sure, ZZ Top were one of a suite of performers at the halftime show in 1997, but everybody there was lip-synching, with ZZ Top going so far as to use the old studio versions of their tracks. Conversely, this was Kiss playing and singing and getting up there and doing it as the only act. There'd be more to follow, with The Rolling Stones, Aerosmith, and The Who, but Kiss were in there on the ground floor. Finally, for one hot minute in 1999, it was more about blowing things up than Up with People.

39
CADILLAC DREAMS
THE KISS-THEMED FEATURE FILM *DETROIT ROCK CITY*

Gene's now decades-long fascination with the movie biz welled up again when a confluence of events had former Kiss photographer Barry Levine shopping a TV movie deal about a bunch of fans hitting various walls as they try to get to see their rock heroes, Kiss. One thing leads to another, and Gene finds himself working (in Ontario, the east end of Toronto and Hamilton, specifically) with writer Carl V. Dupré and director Adam Rifkin on *Detroit Rock City*, a raunchy coming-of-age teen comedy set in 1978 in which four bed-headed Kiss fans from Cleveland get stoned, mugged, and beaten up en route to see Kiss in Detroit. There's sex, vomit, farts, car crashes, convenience store robberies, and nasty clergymen along the way, but also a generous amount of '70s hard rock classics as soundtrack to the high jinks, including the likes of AC/DC, Thin Lizzy, Sweet, Ted Nugent, T. Rex, Styx, Blue Öyster Cult, Golden Earring, Nazareth, and, of course, Kiss.

There are Kiss pinball machines, comic books, and other merch quickly at a glance, and an amusing scene in the smoke-filled Volvo where Christine and the guys are debating the merits of disco (specifically Donna Summer, KC and the Sunshine Band, and Village People), and she says that she wouldn't be surprised if Kiss did a disco song one day. By the way, most of what gets said in that car scene alone wouldn't make it into a movie in our currently much more politically correct times, raunchy teen comedy or otherwise. For proof of how standards have changed, compare *Detroit Rock City* with 2022's *Metal Lords*, for example.

Still, like *Metal Lords*, there are tender moments and in fact near-constant struggles with right or wrong (again, wrong seems to have won out a lot more in 1978 than it does these days). In fact, by the end of the movie, there's more comedy derived from chortles over what one could get away with in 1999 than the actual corny lines designed to make us laugh.

After its #13-ranked August 13, 1999, debut in theaters, *Detroit Rock City* quickly went on to become a box office bomb, grossing about $4 million in U.S. ticket sales and another $2 million internationally against a budget of $17 million, an inordinate amount of that no doubt going to music licensing. It generated a pretty cool soundtrack album, however, featuring heavy hitters like Black Sabbath, Van Halen, and David Bowie, along with Pantera's cover of Ted Nugent's "Cat Scratch Fever" and Everclear doing Thin Lizzy's "Jailbreak." Kiss are represented with "Shout It Out Loud," "Detroit Rock City," and a new assembly-line Diane Warren power ballad called "Nothing Can Keep Me from You."

But the project spelled curtains for the already fragile reunion of the classic lineup. Ace was greatly offended when a scene featuring his daughter Monique was left on the cutting room floor, and Peter was offended that all the songs chosen for the film were numbers written by Paul and Gene. Word also got out that Gene, admirably hands-on throughout the process, minimized the screen time of the "bad boys of Kiss" because they couldn't act.

Promo shot with the cast of *Detroit Rock City* (from left): Giuseppe Andrews, Edward Furlong, James DeBello, and Sam Huntington.

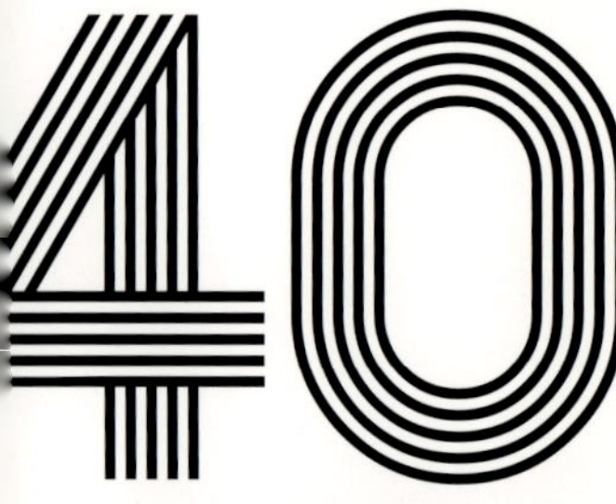

40
YOU WANTED THE BEST
THE BOX SET

If one could accuse Kiss of making a bunch of merch no one needs, well, over on the other side—the studious and academic side—they've regularly risen to the challenge of providing substance. It's taken a while (the guys are busy, right?), but we now have the official *Behind the Mask* biography as well as solid, professional autobiographies from all four of the originals, and more than one book in Gene's case. There are also three volumes of the *Kissology* DVD series, featuring yummy, well-appointed, and sensibly arranged selections from the video archive.

But most impressive of all is *The Box Set*, issued on November 20, 2001, and featuring ninety-four tracks spread over the course of six hours. Past any irritation one might express at the casual approach to titling the thing, this landmark five-CD package finds the band generously and enthusiastically throwing open the doors to the vault, taking fans on an entertaining trawl through the songwriting process, as well as, by extension, the selection process with respect to what makes it onto any given official album. But "you wanted the best," so not only do we get meticulously restored audio, but through the course of a 128-page booklet, the guys offer an extensive oral history of the tracks enclosed, although, granted, Gene and Paul do most of the talking.

Highlights on disc one include actual finished and unreleased Wicked Lester songs (including the band's funky flute-infected version of "She"), a hard-rocking Paul demo from 1966, and a Gene demo from 1969 called "Leeta," which is basically a '50s crooner tune in waltz time—it's refreshing that Gene would let his guard down and let us hear this, showing that he doesn't take himself as seriously as we might think. There are also demo versions of early Kiss songs as well as "Acrobat" (essentially "Love Theme from Kiss") live in 1973. Disc two includes "Doncha Hesitate," "Mad Dog," and "Love Is Blind," each an original that did not morph into another Kiss song.

Disc three is a little underwhelming, offering mostly album tracks and the odd, interesting demo, as is disc four, although "Time Traveler" and "Ain't That Peculiar" (which became *Hot in the Shade*'s "Little Caesar") are worthy party rocking rarities indicative of what Kiss were up to in

the hair metal '80s. There's also the Bryan Adams–like "Let's Put the X in Sex" lest you didn't want to spend the money on *Smashes, Thrashes & Hits*. The highlight on disc five is a happy-making Paul song called "It's My Life." This was first demoed for the *Creatures of the Night* album, only to appear with alterations from Gene on Wendy O. Williams's solo album. The demo we hear is from the *Psycho Circus* sessions, and according to Gene in the booklet, features Paul, Ace, Peter, and himself.

To be sure, the lion's share of *The Box Set* consists of songs from the studio and live albums, but there's much value in the audio beyond that and even more in the extensive liner notes. Since its release in 2001, the availability of rare Kiss songs has exploded on YouTube, lessening the impact of a package like this. In fact, what we've learned is that *The Box Set* barely scratches the surface of what's out there, the sum total of which proves just how hard Kiss worked to make it look so easy.

Throwing open the doors to the vault, Coliseum Arena, Oakland, California.

RAISE YOUR GLASSES

SYMPHONY: ALIVE IV

If having a studio side on *Alive II* wasn't messy enough, here comes *Alive IV*, where even the title is confusing—the cover's got a Kiss logo with the word *Symphony* tucked underneath (first bit of dissonance), then there's *Alive IV* with *2-28-03* tucked underneath, plus a crest with text and the tagline, "Your Presence Is Requested."

It doesn't stop there. The album is partitioned in three, with Act One featuring the oddball lineup of Gene, Paul, Peter, and Tommy Thayer rocking out on six songs, the wrinkles being "Lick It Up" and "Psycho Circus," of interest given the staffing. Act Two features the Melbourne Symphony Ensemble helping the guys with five soft rock numbers, the wrinkles here being obscurities "Sure Know Something" and "Shandi." Then we're on to Act Three, Kiss with the Melbourne Symphony Orchestra collaborating on ten additional numbers, all expected set list staples, save for "Great Expectations." This is actually how the show was sequenced, with the event taking place at the Telstra Dome (now Marvel Stadium) in Melbourne, Australia, on February 28, 2003.

The view from my curmudgeon couch is the same one I had watching Metallica do this: It would have sounded vastly better without the classical folks sawing away. And in this case, it's even creepier because they wore Kiss makeup doing it. To me, this always sounded like a perfectly good Kiss performance with an ersatz

synth or keyboard track, where . . . nice experiment, but cooler heads prevailed and it was removed in the mix. Put another way, it sounds like a perfectly good Kiss performance, but somebody's got a radio on tuned to a classical station and can someone turn that bloody thing off?!

So for a bunch of reasons, this isn't really *Alive IV*, and we may as well pile on one more: What was supposed to be *Alive IV* was in fact something called *The Millennium Concert*. This features Gene, Paul, Ace, and Peter at the height of reunion mania recorded live at BC Place in Vancouver, over New Year's 1999/2000. Label politics squelched the release of the album, but we did eventually get to see it as part of the *Kiss Alive! 1975–2000* box set, issued on November 21, 2006, three years after this Melbourne business, which was issued as a two-CD package on July 22, 2003, followed by a single-disc edition in October of that year. *The Millennium Concert* also saw a two-LP vinyl release in 2014, making it feel even more like the true *Alive IV*. And like the *Symphony* album, there we get a bevy of cool fan curios, namely the original lineup performing "Heaven's on Fire," "Into the Void," "2000 Man," "I Love It Loud," and "Lick It Up."

Still, whichever you choose (and any true Kiss Army private will pick both), the actual *Alive IV* is admirably appointed, naming in the booklet all the symphony players and even all the names of the kids in the Australian Children's Choir, right next to a big fat picture of them all onstage with the Kiss guys. It's a nice touch, and I'm sure serves as a magic memory for those painted-up kids, not to mention the musicians who got to tiptoe through the tulips as the guys blasted their way through "Detroit Rock City" and "God of Thunder."

The sixty-piece Melbourne Symphony Orchestra, wearing black-and-white face paint, perform with the band on February 28, 2003.

42

HOOLIGAN

PETER CRISS TOURS FOR THE LAST TIME AS PART OF KISS

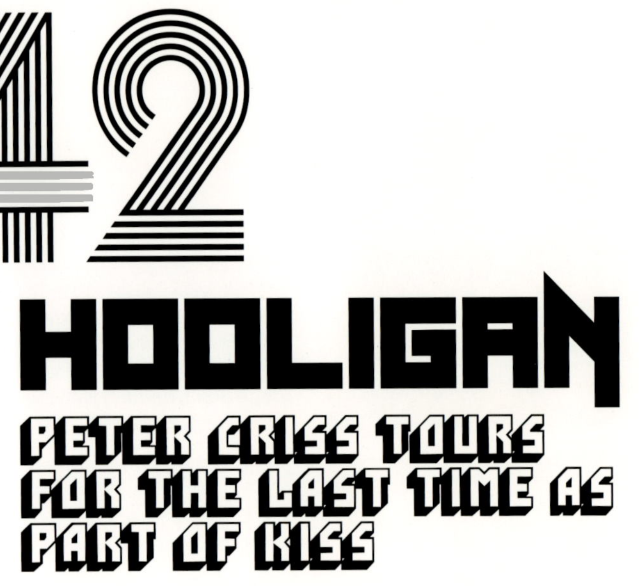

Kiss had already lost Ace for the second time, albeit for the first time during the reunion era. Frehley would play his last show with Kiss on April 12, 2001, at the Carerra Stadium, Gold Coast, Australia, ushering in the Tommy Thayer era that persists to this day.

Peter's departure, on the other hand, is more complicated. Having found out that Ace was getting paid $50,000 per show but himself $10,000 less, Peter lodged a protest by adding a tear to his makeup design. Threatening to quit if his pay wasn't raised to match Ace's, amends were made and the fragile relationship persisted, although nobody was talking to anybody. Finally, frustration came to a head once more, with Peter trashing (more like gingerly tipping over) his drum set at the end of a show in Charleston, South Carolina, on October 7, 2000. Japanese dates in November would be canceled, and the band's spring tour of Japan and Australia in 2001 would feature Peter's replacement, Eric Singer, with Ace still in the band—Paul cracked that Peter's refusal of $1 million to do the clutch of Japanese shows was "a brilliant business decision" on the drummer's part. Do the math, and Charleston therefore represents the last Kiss show featuring the original lineup.

After essentially taking 2000 off, the band returned to full touring duties in the summer 2003, co-headlining with Aerosmith on a traveling show they called *Rocksimus Maximus*. Desperately in need of a third original member and unable to come to terms with Ace, Gene and Paul reluctantly called Peter back. It was a disaster right from the start, with Paul saying that Peter complained about everything: his hotel rooms, the pyro, his hands hurting, the show being too long, and, as always, the money he was being paid. For his part, Peter admitted he complained, stating that he missed Ace and the band just wasn't Kiss without him.

The pairing with Aerosmith was a huge success. Although Kiss went on first, both bands played an eighty-minute set, meaning a compromise between a strident career retrospective and the straight-between-the-eyes nature of a typical thirty-minute support slot. The exclusively American campaign began on August 2 in Hartford, Connecticut, and wound up on December 20 in Fresno, California. Although Peter wasn't fired in Fresno, the show would represent his last, given that his contract with the band would be allowed to expire into 2004, with no new overtures being sent his way.

When the band resumed touring duties in May, first hitting their new home away from home, Australia, followed by Japan and then back to the United States, we'd experience what the guys called "the new Kiss," namely Gene and Paul with Tommy and Eric. Paul quite sensibly likened Kiss to a sports team, saying that when members get traded, the team doesn't fold and the fans keep coming. In the same breath he said, "Somebody is out there who can come in and take my place."

At his end, Peter said a part of him wanted his phone to ring and get asked to come back to work. Now that it hadn't, he'd never been happier—he had the support of family and his wife Gigi, he had his fans, and he had God, and now he could go back to being an artist. True to his word, Peter issued a fifth solo album in 2007 called *One for All*, followed by an autobiography called *Makeup to Breakup: My Life In and Out of Kiss*. And although announcing in 2017 his retirement from touring, five years later, at the age of seventy-six, there he was jumping up onstage at Creatures Fest 2022 both singing and drumming with Ace, the two performing "Hard Luck Woman" and "Strange Ways" like it was old times.

Lakewood Amphitheatre, Atlanta, Georgia. Peter's **2003** return to the band was a disaster from the start.

Brothers in arms, Cricket
Wireless Amphitheatre,
Chula Vista, California,
August 12, 2012.

43

KINGS OF THE NIGHT-TIME WORLD

KISS ARE HONORED AT THE FIRST *VH1 ROCK HONORS*

Even though the *VH1 Rock Honors* ceremony wound up running only from 2006 to 2008, it was a pretty big deal at the time, with excellent production values and a bad boy image designed to knock the stuffing out of the Rock & Roll Hall of Fame. The first one took place at the Mandalay Bay Events Center in Las Vegas on May 25, 2006 (airing six days later), and four hard-rocking acts were being inducted: Queen, Judas Priest, Def Leppard, and Kiss.

Each band's live showcase was preceded by a video montage and a tribute performance. Kiss were feted by an all-star tribute band consisting of huge Kiss fan Scott Ian from Anthrax (playing a signature Gene Simmons Axe Blade bass), along with a couple Guns N' Roses members in Slash and Gilby Clarke. On drums was Tommy Lee of Mötley Crüe and on growly aggressive vocals, Rob Zombie, whose success in the biz owes much to the stage shows pioneered by Kiss in the '70s. Filling out the metal celebrity

Performing at Rock Honors in Las Vegas, Thursday, May 25, 2006.

The God of Thunder and the Metal God Rob Halford at the close of ceremonies.

cast was none other than Ace Frehley (who was kept a surprise), with the lightning-in-a-bottle band performing a slamming version of "God of Thunder."

Come time for the comic book heroes of our story, the band is introduced by actress Natasha Henstridge, who calls Kiss's music "catchy, horny, and hot," adding, "It's the soundtrack to those who want to rock and roll all night, and that's why we always lick it up." Then the guys bound onstage, full show, and perform "Detroit Rock City," "Deuce," and "Love Gun," ending in a massive pyro-scorched windup, after which Natasha joins them onstage and congratulates all the nominees and says good night. The audio is great, offering a pro mix of guitar, bass, drums, and vocals, as is the camerawork, with edits that are perfectly balanced, neither too quick nor too staid. As the credits roll, Kiss are joined by members of Def Leppard and Judas Priest, as well as Brian May, Roger Taylor, and Paul Rodgers, who is seen chatting with Paul Stanley, just after Eric Singer embraces Def Leppard drummer Rick Allen.

In 2007, Ozzy Osbourne, ZZ Top, Heart, and Genesis were celebrated, and in the final year it was all about one band: The Who. But neither ceremony could even match the excitement of the inaugural event, closed by the hottest band in the land. This was indeed an inspired performance, with Paul in particular leaving it all onstage—Gene, Tommy, and Eric are no slouches either—again, manifest mostly in one of the most insane Kiss song closeouts ever kaptured for komprehensive kable konsumption.

44

BLACK DIAMOND

GENE SIMMONS FAMILY JEWELS PREMIERS ON A&E

I'm cognizant we're stepping off the Kissmobile (maybe the only reason we haven't seen one of those is because Hershey's beat Gene to it?) for this particular career milestone, but nonetheless, the hit show *Gene Simmons Family Jewels* did much for the profile of the band, the same way *The Osbournes* boosted Ozzy's fame. But to be fair to the other prime Kisser, Paul's done some admirable things on the side too, including a solo tour in 1989, his *Live to Win* solo album in 2006, his *Paul Stanley's Soul Station* album in 2021, his career as a painter, and, perhaps most impressive of all, starring in the Toronto production of *Phantom of the Opera* in 1999.

The show reveals the exploits of Gene's marriage with Shannon Tweed, along with their two good kids, Nick and Sophie. In fact, Shannon, Nick, and Sophie all come off as well-adjusted, confident, and caring people, while Gene presents a somewhat amped-up version of himself as business polymath, but still with a capacity to laugh at himself or at least view everything around him as amusing. He's also clearly had a good influence on Nick and Sophie, who have both gone to college and turned out great. Both are smart and introspective about Dad's narcissism, which further endears them in the eyes of the viewing public.

Major drama ensues when Gene and Shannon both get face-lifts—it's heartbreaking seeing Sophie cry as she sees her dad transformed, and fans still haven't gotten used to the new Gene fifteen years later. There's also introspection from Gene on his Jewish heritage, culminating in a trip to Israel, plus a cancer scare for Shannon. It gets heavier when Shannon calls Gene on

Gene's and Shannon's kids, Sophie Simmons and Nick Simmons.

his philandering and they look to be on the rocks. Harder to watch than any episode of the show is the couple's appearance on *The Joy Behar Show* in 2011. But as the episodes mount, Gene and Shannon wind up getting married, twenty-eight years after they first started dating, with TV viewers seeing many of the difficult steps along the way. They return to talk with Joy after the October 1, 2011, wedding, and Gene says all the right things.

Only *Dog the Bounty Hunter* was rated higher on A&E through the first couple of seasons of *Gene Simmons Family Jewels,* although its most successful season was the sixth, themed around the couple's poisoned relationship. All told, the show ran for 160 episodes over seven seasons, from August 7, 2006, through January 14, 2012. Despite typical reality TV show editing, resulting in deft sculpting of narratives (and even the odd full-on fib), by the end of the series, the personalities of these four people were laid bare for all to see, with each of them complex, grappling, reconciling, and fighting through intense psychological dramas, if also obviously not hurting for material wealth and the unencumbered enjoyment thereof.

Nick, Shannon, Sophie, and Gene are interviewed at the Geffen Playhouse, Westwood, California, May 5, 2006.

45
ROCKET RIDE

SONIC BOOM, FEATURING NEW GUITARIST TOMMY THAYER

As if finally and self-consciously aware that the band has not delivered a new album in more than a decade, Kiss react and correct with a value proposition. But this had to happen for other reasons as well. In 2009 (or let's say 2005 to 2012), the industry was going through its most heated battles against downloading, of which the most virulent strain was free downloading. *Sonic Boom*, issued on October 6, 2009, is a pointed product of this era, offering swell and swollen digipak packaging, a good long album, a second disc featuring fully fifteen rerecorded Kiss hits, and a third disc, a DVD, featuring six songs shot live in Buenos Aires. Also a trend in retailing during this era, the album was sold in the United States and Canada exclusively at Walmart and for a nice price. All of this was coupled with Gene railing in the press about the immorality of free music.

And where it mattered most, across the album's eleven new originals, Kiss delivered exactly what fans wanted: an ambitious batch of well-performed and exquisitely recorded songs that celebrated the Kiss sound of yore. Which is a little different, because a lot of old bands suddenly went "smart," trying to compete with younger bands making classic hard rock. *Sonic Boom* doesn't do that. The lyrics are good ol'/same ol' Kiss, the chords are kept to a minimum, and even at eleven songs, they stayed restrained.

In fact, opening single "Modern Day Delilah," issued two months before the full album, was a bit of a fake-out, being uncharacteristically complicated and heavy, even weighty (Paul says it was inspired by "I Want You," which makes sense). Fans loved it, but then the balance of the record was closer to comfort food, with the outliers being left for the end of the record: "Danger Us" has a "Deuce" vibe, "Say Yeah" is heavy '80s arena rock, and "I'm an Animal" is something that would fit on Black Sabbath's *13* album. Elsewhere, Tommy sings "When Lightning Strikes" and Eric sings "All for the Glory," but both of these fit the happy-making '70s Kiss mandate of about seven of the album's songs, inspired perhaps by *Revenge* and that record's work ethic. Fans were quick to point out that "Never Enough" bore a resemblance to Poison's "Nothin' But a Good Time," but then again, both of them bear a resemblance to Elton John's "Saturday Night's All Right for Fighting" and Kiss's own "Shout It Out Loud." Also adding to the idea of going back to the band's roots—Paul made no qualms about that in interviews—was

the use of Michael Doret for the cover art, who served up something similar to what he did for *Rock and Roll Over*.

Of interest in the credits is the fact that we see three Paul and Gene cowrites, along with five solo credits, with Tommy entering into the mix as well, three times. Paul is listed as the producer, with Greg Collins (U2, No Doubt, Matchbox 20) given a coproducer credit. Whoever did the heavy lifting, the album sounds vibrant and bright, emphasizing snare and cymbals, with everything else sitting nicely in the mix. The backup vocals are a little fakey, but that's a small complaint, especially given how both Paul and Gene on leads project their personalities with aplomb. All told, the theme was teamwork like the old days, with the band writing together (and with no one from the outside), playing together as much as possible, and

using vintage gear, with Paul capturing the whole thing analog before the tapes were turned over for processing through ProTools.

Not that video meant much by this point, but a nice clip was produced for "Modern Day Delilah," featuring live footage artfully edited, but also at the front and back, realistic portrayals of the four Kiss guys as giants bounding through modern-day Detroit. Still, it didn't have much effect on the single's chart performance, and the album as a whole debuted disappointingly at about 108,000 copies in its first week, although that had doubled by the end of the year, with *Sonic Boom* now sitting at about 325,000 copies sold—weirdly, it's still not available on Spotify or other streaming services.

46

GETAWAY
KISS LAUNCH THEIR FIRST *KISS KRUISE*

Never wanting to be left out, Kiss were pretty early on involved in the rock cruise industry, conducting their first Kiss Kruise, sailing on the Carnival Destiny from the Port of Miami on October 13, 2011, and returning four days later. The band performed electrically and acoustically, having been conditioned for intimate shows through the convention and *MTV Unplugged* projects. Fans were treated to super-deep tracks like "Just a Boy," "Mr. Blackwell," and "I" (albeit all partial), and from the really old days, "Anything for My Baby." Some of the *MTV Unplugged* material hadn't been played since 1995. "Getaway" and "Comin' Home" were played fully electric for the first time ever as well.

About two thousand fans were assembled for a seventy-five-minute unplugged show upon the five o'clock sailing on the 13th, after which the band took an hour's worth of questions. Next was an electric show in the Palladium Lounge with capacity topping off at about one thousand, everybody more or less taken care of through a first and second show (the 14th and 15th, respectively), where the band admirably changed up the set list. Both shows were simulcast up to screens on the pool deck.

Also included were a pajama party, a Halloween party, a showing of *Detroit Rock City*, Kiss trivia and karaoke, Kasino Night with Eric Singer, miniature golf with Tommy Thayer, a tattoo contest, and pictures taken with the band. Reports had Sixthman, the company running things, proving capable and enthusiastic about their work.

The lineup for the inaugural Kiss Kruise included the heroes of our story along with Skid Row, Bad City, The Envy, Craig Gass, Big Rock Show, Brian Collins, and Radiolucent. There has been one every year since, except for 2020. The 2012 and 2013 editions weren't much more star-studded than the first one, but 2014 included Cheap Trick, The Pat Travers Band, and The Dead Daisies. Steel Panther, Lita Ford, and Fozzy played in 2015, with The Dead Daisies returning. The 2016 edition included the short-lived reunion of Whitford St. Holmes along with Skid Row, King's X, and Enuff Znuff, while 2017 featured Extreme. In 2018, Ace Frehley and Bruce Kulick climbed aboard, with Bruce returning the following year, joined by Warrant and The Darkness. In 2021, Kiss were joined by Night Ranger, Queensrÿche, Sebastian Bach, and Tommy's old bad Black 'n Blue. And then it grows: 2022's Kiss Kruise XI, split between the two weeks, featured Dokken, Warrant, LA Guns, Lita Ford, Bruce Kulick, Black Label Society, Buckcherry, Stryper, and Vixen—all aboard!

REFLECTIONS ON THE KISS KAST

"I think I'll leave that to other people to answer," laughs Paul, about the differences between himself and cast member Gene Simmons when it comes to songwriting. "I think clearly over the years, the style and the way of writing became very clearly individual. And I would leave that to others to decide, you know, their viewpoint. Obviously, I have my songs of Gene's that I'm more fond of than others. And I think that perhaps a major difference is that

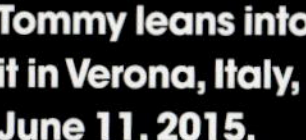

Tommy leans into
it in Verona, Italy,
June 11, 2015.

As for the casting of members for the Kiss show when it comes to the six-stringers, Paul figures, "Well, clearly, I think that the viewpoint of the band, musically, has always been based on the rhythm guitar. The school of writing came from my playing, so I can only write what I could play and what I liked playing. I think that Ace and I together . . . I used to talk about the one big guitar—that's what we wanted to be. I was always a big fan of two guitars playing different voicings, but sometimes, in listening to them, not being able to tell anything other than there was one big guitar. So I thought Ace and I, in the beginning, were everything I wanted that to be. I enjoyed that tremendously, and again, the idea was to try to maintain that as we went forward.

"As we lost a member, the idea was to not change the band, but continue where we left off as much as possible. Bruce is and was a great guitar player. I would say that the biggest challenge, perhaps, for him, was to play like we play and like I play, and to forgo some of the frills and chops for attitude and passion. Sometimes technical prowess can get in the way of some of that gut-level feel. And with Bruce it was a matter of trying to keep his knowledge and ability in check."

Paul continues, "Tommy is much more . . . Tommy is a great, fabulous, you know, blows-me-away kind of guitar player. And he's also closer to being a rock guitar player in the sense that I would have to say I prefer. Tommy can blow me away on any night, with what he's playing, and incidentally, the guitar players in other bands who are at the shows are knocked out sometimes—beyond impressed— with what Tommy can do as a guitar player. And he, in all the best senses, maintains the style and personality, and also raises the bar, which is not easy to do."

Finally, part of being in a cast is compatibility. I asked Paul if he found it odd that in the beginning, Kiss seemed to have these two highly disciplined guys, and then a couple of firecrackers, and whether that was ideal. Delicately asked, the question got a delicate answer.

"Ideal has to do with compatibility," Paul begins, "but it also has a lot to do with combustibility. Ideal doesn't necessarily mean smooth. Certainly in the beginning, what helped create Kiss was this, I guess, disparity and the divergence of opinions. The only thing that needed to be harnessed, always, were those talents and those personalities. And that took the two more disciplined people to do."

Eric Carr, 1980
(main) and Eric
Singer 2019 (below).

47

ALMOST HUMAN
MONSTER

If *Sonic Boom* was a case of getting the mandate for *Psycho Circus* right, mission accomplished. But Paul—and it really is Paul running things at this point—decided that was then and this is now, very sensibly saying that if anybody out there had sidled up to *Sonic Boom*, the band's twentieth studio album, *Monster*, issued on October 9, 2012, was that record on steroids.

It's the perfect analogy. Not only are the songs on *Monster* uniformly heavier—and yet still weirdly demonstrative of things Kiss might do in the '70s and '80s—the sound of the thing is positively huge. Paul specifically went for a more distorted tone out of Gene, but the big difference is in Eric's drums, which sound like cannons. And then there's Tommy Thayer, who figures into the songwriting on nine out of twelve tracks. Tommy has acknowledged his stamp on the album, and I guess that stamp is that he likes heavy Gene-styled Kiss songs, wide-angled, lumbering, pounded home, as well as happier things as long as they're heavy.

Lead single "Hell or Hallelujah" kicks things off, with Paul writing an up-tempo rocker evocative of "I Stole Your Love." It's a better single than last time out and a real call to arms, banging off of the bricks with Tommy firing off high-octane licks at every turn. "Wall of Sound" is next, and it's an apt descriptive for Paul's approach as a whole—Kiss almost went with this as the title of the album. "Freak" follows, and this one is the biggest departure from the relentless power presented; it's a glammy song with a lot of melody, and the guys got close to making it a duet with Lady Gaga.

Like last time, Tommy and Eric each take a lead vocal. Tommy's song, "Outta This World," is a true *Sonic Boom* rocker muscled up and then whacked with cowbell. If Tommy was tentative the first time out, he blossoms here, singing like Ace but with a cleaner, more soulful voice. Eric sings "All for the Love of Rock & Roll," which oldsters may recognize as substantially similar to the Tuff Darts' song of the same name, issued on that band's debut from 1978 but first covered by Ram Jam in 1977. Paul takes a sole credit on the song, which is puzzling. The main theory is that Paul paid for the rights to take the credit, although unlike when this usually happens, the song is a known quantity. Still, there are notable differences, most significantly with the lyrics.

Elsewhere, Gene sings "Back to the Stone Age" and "The Devil in Me," a couple of metal-munchers, and he

plays like John Entwistle on "Shout Mercy," possibly the best song across these two albums, modern-day surprises from Kiss that are recorded by the same production team using some of the same studio space and some of the same vintage gear but sounding unalike.

But if the sonic palette is different, and if the general complexion of *Monster* is more raucous and unbridled than the sum of *Sonic Boom*, then there's still crossover in terms of party songs like "Eat Your Heart Out," "Take Me Down Below," "Last Chance," and the songs capably manhandled by Tommy and Eric. Bottom line, this is the best version of Kiss, but it's still Kiss—as Spinal Tap sagely put it, "It's such a fine line between clever and stupid"— essentially an evolution from *Revenge* and *Sonic Boom*, skipping the two in between.

If *Monster* is the last studio album Kiss ever do (and it's definitely looking that way), then they certainly have bowed out if not the hottest band in the land, then literally the hottest, loudest, and proudest they themselves have ever played and been recorded. And it's a shame that all those things both Paul and Gene said about new music from classic rock bands being ignored and irrelevant turned out to be accurate. *Monster* fell far short of gold, selling one hundred thousand fewer copies than its predecessor. Mind you, outside of the nifty lenticular front cover art, the album lacked the extras added onto *Sonic Boom*. Nor did Gene and Paul persist in selling the album live—by this point, band and fans alike had begun to realize that the legacy was just too long and rich to be taking new songs to heart.

Bringing the unbridled *Monster* to the Sweden Rock Festival, Norje, Solvesborg, Sweden, June 6, 2013.

The band arrives at the 47th Annual Academy of Country Music Awards at the MGM Hotel in Las Vegas, Nevada, April 1, 2012.

MGM G
Canon

THE TOUR
KISS
MOTLEY CRUE
WORKING

THE TOUR
KISS
MOTLEY CRUE
WORKING

THE TOUR
KISS
MOTLEY CRUE
WORKING

THE TOUR
KISS
MOTLEY CRUE
WORKING

48

ALL THE WAY

KISS ARE INDUCTED INTO THE ROCK & ROLL HALL OF FAME

Van Halen, Guns N' Roses, and Deep Purple had contentious Rock & Roll Hall of Fame inductions, and then who can forget Steve Miller's rant, which was more so about the dirty secret of the cost to the artists of getting in. Add Blondie, Creedence Clearwater Revival, and Chicago to the brew and it's almost expected that bands with long histories pack their baggage and bring it to New York, where most of the in-person stuff takes place before these embattled rock warriors are permanently recognized on the windy shores of Lake Erie.

Kiss got off light in the end. First, there had been resentment that the band had been eligible since 1999 but it took until 2014 for them to get in, Kiss entering the Hall along with Nirvana, Peter Gabriel, Linda Ronstadt, Cat Stevens, Hall and Oates, and The E Street Band in a ceremony that took place on April 10 at the Barclay Center in Brooklyn. Rush had been inducted the previous year, and just like Kiss in 2014, it was put down to vociferous fan support that they got the nod. In fact, the narrative has now ossified that Rush and Kiss represent the first two cases for which the roar of the mob was loud enough to force the hand of Jann Wenner and the dismissive cabal generally thought to go with more critic-friendly and politically correct choices over voices. Paul said as much during his perfunctory speech, defiantly, forcefully, but also tactfully and quickly, walking up to the line but not crossing it.

But it started with the longest of the speeches, from Rage Against the Machine guitarist Tom Morello, a huge Kiss fan since youth, who came at the idea from many angles that it was uncool to like Kiss, but after all these years, against critical (and school bully) resistance, the Kiss Army had been proven right.

Gene was second to speak, and if anything, he smoothed any ruffled feathers, sounding grateful and gracious, using the word "humbled" three times. Peter spoke next, nicely taking care of business, thanking Bill Aucoin and his wife Gigi and telling the crowd that he was now seven years male breast cancer-free. He also mentioned that he had taken his first drum lesson from "his best friend, Jerry Nolan of The New York Dolls" and, most contentiously, that "even out of makeup, I'll always be the Catman." Ace looked like he was going to burst out of his suit, but he did great as well, responsibly thanking a number of people back at the original Kiss office along with family. He also included a message about sobriety, escaping the speech unscathed, much to the relief of Paul and Gene.

And then it was up to Paul to make the aforementioned point about getting into the Rock Hall because of the fans, while also acknowledging the significance of "the original four," but not forgetting to mention Bruce, Tommy, and Eric. He then made a point about seeing his rock heroes live and that the spirit of rock 'n' roll embodied within them had much to do with following one's own path. After saying that's what Kiss had done for forty years, he delivered this barb: "Here we are tonight, basically inducted for the same things that we were kept out for," referring to the fifteen years kept outside the Hall.

The final protest was one of omission: Kiss did not perform, ticked off for the above reasons but also a secondary dispute, the age-old debate over which members of a band should be inducted. As with most acts, if you start including more people, you get to gray-area cases. We need not get into a discussion of this band's "gene" pool of ten—Simmons mentioned them all and therefore dutifully put the entire cast on the record. But the problem was heightened when it came to the idea of performance. Gene and Paul were on the outs with Ace and Peter. Plus, the current vigorous version of the band consisted of Gene, Paul, Tommy, and Eric, with there being

doubts that Peter could even perform at this point. And with the size of the Kiss show being part and parcel of why they were there in the first place, it seemed easier not to go through all that hassle.

In the end, the original four members of Kiss would make do with their short and sweet speeches. Although at least in theory, they got the building renamed in their honor. "I misspoke earlier when I said that tonight Kiss enters the Rock & Roll Hall of Fame," quipped Morello at the end of his endearing treatise. "That's *almost* right. Because tonight it's not the Rock & Roll Hall of Fame. Tonight, it's the Rock and Roll All Nite and Party Every Day Hall of Fame."

The proud Hall inductees, Paul, Peter, Ace, and Gene.

WHEN LIGHTNING STRIKES

SETTING THE MARK FOR MOST GOLD RECORDS BY AN AMERICAN BAND

On September 15, 2015, Kiss were given an award by the Record Industry Association of America declaring them the American band with the most RIAA-certified gold records, citing thirty in total, twenty-six as Kiss plus the four 1978 solo albums. Sales-wise, Kiss doesn't even crack the top one hundred, and if we count Elvis Presley, Garth Brooks, and George Strait as American "bands," well, then, Kiss are at minimum fourth, with those guys having as many or more platinum albums than Kiss have gold. Outside of America, The Beatles have more gold albums, but again, there are various ways to cook this one, including total U.S. record sales or any version of worldwide sales, including raw numbers or worldwide gold and platinum awards.

Still, it's quite an achievement, especially considering that twenty-one of those thirty are studio albums, along with the fact that the band is ripe for a new round of certification inquiries that, given the new math of streaming, should reveal a few more plateaus reached. Where Kiss fall short is that they've never had the monster hit record that went diamond or even halfway to diamond, which many bands at this level—such as Aerosmith, AC/DC, Heart, Whitesnake, Mötley Crüe, and Def Leppard—have had somewhere along the trajectory. In a similar camp to Kiss would be the likes of Blue Öyster Cult, Cheap Trick, Foghat, Judas Priest, and Scorpions, but even Deep Purple, Black Sabbath, David Bowie, and Rush, who, granted, saw *Moving Pictures* certify as five times platinum as late as April 19, 2021. Let this be a lesson to those counting Kiss albums: There is very likely more official sales success out there to be found and documented for all time, which one would think would be important to achievers like Gene and Paul. Bottom line, there's really no easier relatable success metric than the language of gold and platinum records. To be sure, it might be even easier to say you've made it into the Rock & Roll Hall of Fame or have a certain number of Grammys, but neither of those says as much as RIAA certifications, especially with moderate to committed music fans.

In any event, the band's label, Universal, made sure to play up this highly qualified announcement, with Sujata Murthy and Meg McLean Corso writing in a press release that said, "Kiss remains one of the most influential bands in the history of rock 'n' roll. Decades of record-breaking tours around the globe have included high-profile appearances at Super Bowl XXXIII, the Winter Olympics in Salt Lake City, the *Rockin' the Corps* concert dedicated to our troops in Iraq and Afghanistan, special guest appearance on the 2009 *American Idol* finale that boasted thirty million viewers, and a 2010 Dr Pepper Super Bowl commercial and advertising campaign in support of their *Hottest Show on Earth* tour." Also in the press release was a message from chairman and CEO of RIAA, who said, "What an extraordinary achievement for an enduring band. Forty years later and the band is still rocking. Congratulations to Kiss on their gold album milestone and continued success."

"I want you!" O2 Arena, Berlin, Germany, June 3, 2015.

The *End of the Road* reaches
**West Palm Beach, Florida,
September 21, 2022.**

To any member of the Kiss Army at the profound end of getting older, what's most inspiring from Kiss—beyond the late-career entry into the Rock Hall and beyond being celebrated for thirty gold records—has been the enormity of the band's farewell tour. Or the second farewell tour, I should say, a sprawling and long goodbye called *End of the Road World Tour*.

It began on January 31, 2019, at the Rogers Arena in beautiful Vancouver, British Columbia, with the plan for the campaign announced after the band's performance of "Detroit Rock City" on *America's Got Talent*. What ensued was one of the band's sharpest productions, presented throughout North America and Europe, closed out by five Japanese dates in December of that year.

As we crossed into 2020, the organization was unrelenting, Gene, Paul, Tommy, and Eric playing most of February and into mid-March, at which point everything lurched to a halt because of the worldwide coronavirus pandemic. After a period of silence and confusion in the music business, bands began playing on YouTube and at drive-ins. But then trust Kiss to deliver at the highest level, coming up with a "New Year's Eve Goodbye 2020" pay-for-view livestream concert—recorded in Dubai, no less—followed by a well-regarded official rock documentary called *Biography: Kisstory*. After the premiere at the Tribeca Film Festival on June 11, 2021, the band treated the crowd to a five-song set in Battery Park. Somehow Kiss managed to stay in the spotlight, even if the surprise studio album that other bands cooked up on the downtime wasn't to be part of this band's particular plan.

Also not part of the plan was the soft retirement we saw with other bands once the doors to the world's concert halls were flung open after the bug was tamed. Instead, Kiss hauled their heavy costumes up onstage once again, beginning August 18, 2021, just outside of Boston, with the guys proceeding to smack America hard on the lips through to a last U.S. tour leg show on October 16th in Chicago.

Then it was off to South America in April and May 2022, followed by a short American leg at the end of May and a major European campaign in June and July. A last goodbye to Australia was next, followed by more American dates and a show each in Japan and Mexico. Yet another South American campaign was slated for April 2023, followed by Europe and then, commencing October 20, the final North American leg of the very last tour.

As of this writing, Kiss plans to close out their career at Madison Square Garden over two nights, December 1–2, 2023, which, as Paul reflected, was only fitting, representing a sense of coming "full circle."

"Kiss is much more than a rock 'n' roll band," said Stanley, as quoted in the *End of the Road* tour book. "The band and its fans are a tribe. It's humbling for me that we can be the magnet that brings people together. What we have with the fans is reciprocity. The fans are our oxygen; they are our blood. They make it possible for us to exist."

And that's the way it's been for what is exactly fifty years in 2023, across the fifty milestones we've documented in this book and more. The Kiss Army, with its fanatical devotion, encyclopedic knowledge of the band, and—always, always—the heated debates, has forever been part of the expansive Kiss narrative, whether through the conventions, the many books on the band, and now the myriad YouTube shows dissecting and bisecting the catalog on a seemingly weekly basis. Kiss thanks us and we thank them, in the creation of a feedback loop that has created one of the great rock 'n' roll ecosystems of all time. Bottom line: There will never be a fan network quite like this, because there will never be another band quite like Kiss.

Gene and Paul perform during the band's *End of the Road* tour in Columbia, South Carolina, on February 11, 2020.

DISCOGRAPHY

Concerning a few points on format, I've included an additional notes section for anything I thought was interesting and, er, notable. There are quote marks around songs everywhere except in the track list proper, just to keep things tidy. I've noted side 1/side 2 designations for all releases from the vinyl era, which I've always maintained ends in 1990 (trust me, I was there). Only the most substantial of guest musician credits are noted, and we're not getting into when any of the guitarists play bass and vice versa—some of this extra musician credit stuff, when deemed important, is discussed in the entries. Information on live albums and compilations is cut back here (writing credits, timings on compilations, etc.). That decision was taken to reduce redundancy, not to mention the fact that the live albums in particular are well discussed elsewhere in the book.

Finally, I've included the 1978 solo albums because they are considered by most fans to be part of the Kiss program (plus they say Kiss right on them). It also created a handy space—namely the notes section—to mention what else the four originals got up to solowise throughout their careers, although I've begged off listing the myriad musicians playing on these four concurrently released records.

A.
STUDIO ALBUMS

KISS

Released on February 18, 1974; Casablanca NBLP 7001.

Recorded October–November 1973 at Bell Sound, New York, NY.

Produced by Kenny Kerner and Richie Wise.

Side 1: 1. Strutter (Stanley/Simmons) 3:10; 2. Nothin' to Lose (Simmons) 3:26; 3. Firehouse (Stanley) 3:18; 4. Cold Gin (Frehley) 4:21; 5. Let Me Know (Stanley) 2:58.

Side 2: 1. Kissin' Time (Kal Mann/Bernie Lowe) 3:52; 2. Deuce (Simmons) 3:05; 3. Love Theme from Kiss (Stanley/Simmons/Criss/Frehley) 2:24; 4. 100,000 Years (Stanley/Simmons) 3:22; 5. Black Diamond (Stanley) 5:11.

Notes: Original band lineup consists of Paul Stanley—rhythm guitar and vocals; Ace Frehley—lead guitar and vocals; Gene Simmons—bass and vocals; Peter Criss—drums and vocals. "Kissin' Time" was not included on the original February release of the album; it was recorded in April and added to subsequent releases beginning in July 1974.

HOTTER THAN HELL

Released on October 22, 1974; Casablanca NBLP 7006.

Recorded August 1974 at The Village, Los Angeles, CA.

Produced by Kenny Kerner and Richie Wise.

Side 1: 1. Got to Choose (Stanley) 3:52; 2. Parasite (Frehley) 3:01; 3. Goin' Blind (Simmons/Stephen Coronel) 3:34; 4. Hotter Than Hell (Stanley) 3:30; 5. Let Me Go, Rock 'n' Roll (Stanley/Simmons) 2:16.

Side 2: 1. All the Way (Simmons) 3:17; 2. Watchin' You (Simmons) 3:45; 3. Mainline (Stanley) 3:50; 4. Comin' Home (Stanley/Frehley) 2:37; 5. Strange Ways (Frehley) 3:17.

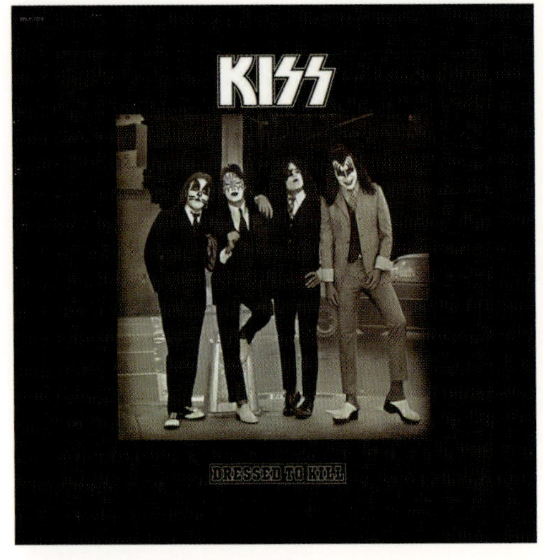

DRESSED TO KILL

Released on March 19, 1975; Casablanca NBLP 7016.

Recorded February 1975 at Electric Lady, New York, NY.

Produced by Neil Bogart and Kiss.

Side 1: 1. Room Service (Stanley) 2:58; 2. Two Timer (Simmons) 2:59; 3. Ladies in Waiting (Simmons) 2:47; 4. Getaway (Frehley) 2:45; 5. Rock Bottom (Intro: Frehley/Stanley) 3:55.

Side 2: 1. C'mon and Love Me (Stanley) 2:54; 2. Anything for My Baby (Stanley) 2:30; 3. She (Simmons/Stephen Coronel) 4:05; 4. Love Her All I Can (Stanley) 2:43; 5. Rock and Roll All Nite (Stanley/Simmons) 2:45.

DESTROYER

Released on March 15, 1976; Casablanca NBLP 7025.

Recorded on September 3–6, 1975, and January–February 1976 at Electric Lady and Record Plant, New York, NY.

Produced by Bob Ezrin.

Side 1: 1. Detroit Rock City (Stanley/Bob Ezrin) 5:30; 2. King of the Night Time World (Kim Fowley/Mark Anthony/Stanley/Ezrin) 3:15; 3. God of Thunder (Stanley) 4:20; 4. Great Expectations (Simmons/Ezrin) 4:20.

Side 2: 1. Flaming Youth (Frehley/Stanley/Simmons/Ezrin) 2:55; 2. Sweet Pain (Simmons) 3:20; 3. Shout It Out Loud (Simmons/Stanley/Ezrin) 2:50; 4. Beth (Criss/Stan Penridge/Ezrin) 2:45; 5. Do You Love Me (Fowley/Ezrin/Stanley) 3:33.

Notes: Additional guitar by Dick Wagner on "Flaming Youth," "Sweet Pain," and "Beth." Orchestration by H. A. Macmillan. Piano on "Beth" and assorted keyboards by Bob Ezrin. The orchestra on "Beth" is the New York Philharmonic.

ROCK AND ROLL OVER

Released on November 11, 1976; Casablanca NBLP 7037.

Recorded September–October 1976 at Star Theatre, Nanuet, NY.

Produced by Eddie Kramer.

Side 1: 1. I Want You (Stanley) 3:02; 2. Take Me (Stanley/Sean Delaney) 2:53; 3. Calling Dr. Love (Simmons) 3:41; 4. Ladies Room (Simmons) 3:25; 5. Baby Driver (Criss/Stan Penridge) 3:39.

Side 2: 1. Love 'Em and Leave 'Em (Simmons) 3:41; 2. Mr. Speed (Stanley/Delaney) 3:19; 3. See You in Your Dreams (Simmons) 2:31; 4. Hard Luck Woman (Stanley) 3:32; 5. Makin' Love (Stanley/Delaney) 3:12.

LOVE GUN

Released on June 30, 1977; Casablanca NBLP 7057.

Recorded May 1977 at Record Plant, New York, NY.

Produced by Kiss and Eddie Kramer.

Side 1: 1. I Stole Your Love (Stanley) 3:04; 2. Christine Sixteen (Simmons) 2:52; 3. Got Love for Sale (Simmons) 3:28; 4. Shock Me (Frehley) 4:17; 5. Tomorrow and Tonight (Stanley) 3:38.

Side 2: 1. Love Gun (Stanley) 3:27; 2. Hooligan (Criss/Stan Penridge) 2:58; 3. Almost Human (Simmons) 2:52; 4. Plaster Caster (Simmons) 2:30; 5. Then She Kissed Me (Jeff Barry/Ellie Greeenwich/Phillip Spector) 2:58.

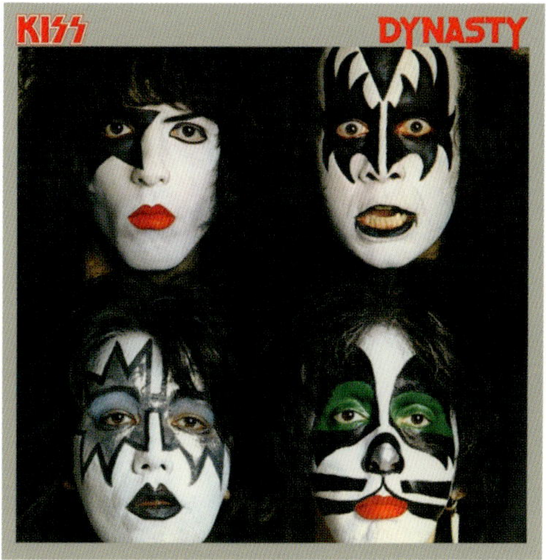

DYNASTY

Released on May 23, 1979; Casablanca NBLP 7152.

Recorded January–February 1979 at Electric Lady and Record Plant, New York, NY.

Produced by Vini Poncia.

Side 1: 1. I Was Made for Lovin' You (Stanley/ Vini Poncia/Desmond Child) 4:29; 2. 2000 Man (Mick Jagger/Keith Richards) 4:53; 3. Sure Know Something (Stanley/Poncia) 3:59; 4. Dirty Livin' (Criss/Poncia/Stan Pendridge) 4:16.

Side 2: 1. Charisma (Simmons/Howard Marks) 4:26; 2. Magic Touch (Stanley) 4:40; 3. Hard Times (Frehley) 3:29; 4. X-Ray Eyes (Simmons) 3:42; 5. Save Your Love (Frehley) 4:39.

Notes: Drums on all tracks except for "Dirty Livin'" are by Anton Fig.

UNMASKED

Released on May 20, 1980; NBLP 7225.

Recorded January–March 1980 at Record Plant, New York, NY.

Produced by Vini Poncia.

Side 1: 1. Is That You? (Gerald McMahon) 3:55; 2. Shandi (Stanley/Vini Poncia) 3:33; 3. Talk to Me (Frehley) 4:00; 4. Naked City (Simons/Bob Kulick/Peppy Castro/Poncia) 3:49; 5. What Makes the World Go 'Round (Stanley/Poncia) 4:14.

Side 2: 1. Tomorrow (Stanley/Poncia) 3:16; 2. Two Sides of the Coin (Frehley) 3:15; 3. She's So European (Simmons/Poncia) 3:30; 4. Easy as It Seems (Stanley/Poncia) 3:24; 5. Torpedo Girl (Frehley/Poncia) 3:31; 6. You're All That I Want (Simmons/Poncia) 3:04.

Notes: All drums by Anton Fig, although official lineup has not changed.

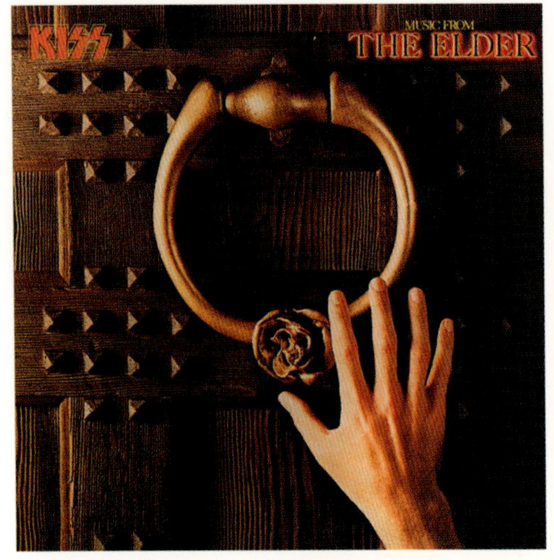

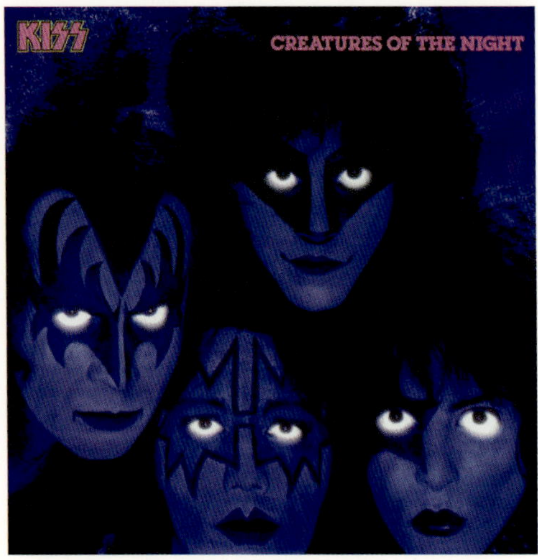

MUSIC FROM THE ELDER

Released on November 10, 1981; Casablanca NBLP 7261.

Recorded March–September 1981 at Ace in the Hole Studios, Wilton, CT; A&R and Record Plant, New York, NY; Sound Exchange, Toronto, Canada; and Ezrin Farm, King City, Canada.

Produced by Bob Ezrin.

Side 1: 1. The Oath (Stanley/Bob Ezrin/Tony Powers) 4:32; 2. Fanfare (Ezrin/Stanley) 1:22; 3. Just a Boy (Stanley/Ezrin) 2:30; 4. Dark Light (Frehley/Anton Fig/Lou Reed/Simmons) 4:12; 5. Only You (Simmons) 4:19; 6. Under the Rose (Carr/Simmons) 4:49.

Side 2: 1. A World Without Heroes (Stanley/ Ezrin/Reed/Simmons) 2:40; 2. Mr. Blackwell (Simmons/Reed) 4:53; 3. Escape from the Island (Frehley/Ezrin/Carr) 2:50; 4. Odyssey (Powers) 5:36; 5. I (Simmons/Ezrin) 3:52; 6. Finale (Stanley/Simmons/Frehley/Carr) 1:04.

Notes: Drummer Peter Criss has been replaced by Eric Carr.

CREATURES OF THE NIGHT

Released on October 28, 1982; Casablanca/ Polygram NBLP 7270.

Recorded July–September 1982 at Record Plant and Record One, Los Angeles, CA, and Media Sound at New York City, NY.

Produced by Michael James Jackson, Paul Stanley, and Gene Simmons.

Side 1: 1. Creatures of the Night (Stanley/ Adam Mitchell) 4:01; 2. Saint and Sinner (Simmons/Mikel Japp) 4:50; 3. Keep Me Comin' (Stanley/Mitchell) 4:00; 4. Rock and Roll Hell (Simmons/Bryan Adams/Jim Vallance) 4:08; 5. Danger (Stanley/Mitchell) 3:55.

Side 2: 1. I Love It Loud (Simmons/Vincent Cusano) 4:12; 2. I Still Love You (Stanley/ Cusano) 6:06; 3. Killer (Simmons/Cusano) 3:19; 4. War Machine (Simmons/Adams/Vallance) 4:13.

Notes: Ace Frehley doesn't play on the album although he is still listed as being part of the band. Most significant session player is Vinnie "Vincent Cusano" Vincent, who will be made an official member in time for the next album.

LICK IT UP

Released on September 23, 1983; Mercury 422-814 297-1 M-1.

Recorded July–August 1983 at Right Track Recording, Record Plant, Atlantic Studios, and The Hit Factory, New York, NY.

Produced by Michael James Jackson, Gene Simmons, and Paul Stanley.

Side 1: 1. Exciter (Stanley/Vinnie Vincent) 4:10; 2. Not for the Innocent (Simmons/Vincent) 4:32; 3. Lick It Up (Stanley/Vincent) 3:59; 4. Young and Wasted (Simmons/Vincent) 4:04; 5. Gimme More (Stanley/Vincent) 3:41.

Side 2: 1. All Hell's Breakin' Loose (Carr/ Stanley/Vincent/Simmons) 4:34; 2. A Million to One (Stanley/Vincent) 4:17; 3. Fits Like a Glove (Simmons) 4:04; 4. Dance All Over Your Face (Simmons) 4:13; 5. And on the 8th Day (Simmons/Vincent) 4:02.

Notes: Guitarist Vinnie Vincent replaces Ace Frehley.

ANIMALIZE

Released on September 13, 1984; Mercury 422-822 495-1 M-1.

Recorded May–July 1984 at Right Track Recording, New York, NY.

Produced by Paul Stanley.

Side 1: 1. I've Had Enough (Into the Fire) (Stanley/Desmond Child) 3:50; 2. Heaven's on Fire (Stanley/Child) 3:18; 3. Burn Bitch Burn (Simmons) 4:38; 4. Get All You Can Take (Stanley/Mitch Weissman) 3:42; 5. Lonely Is the Hunter (Simmons) 4:27.

Side 2: 1. Under the Gun (Stanley/Carr/ Child) 3:59; 2. Thrills in the Night (Stanley/ Jean Beauvoir) 4:18; 3. While the City Sleeps (Simmons/Weissman) 3:39; 4. Murder in High-Heels (Simmons/Weissman) 3:51.

Notes: Guitarist Mark St. John replaces Vinnie Vincent.

ASYLUM

Released on September 16, 1985; Mercury 422-826 099-1 M-1.

Recorded June–July 1985 at Electric Lady and Right Track, New York, NY.

Produced by Paul Stanley and Gene Simmons.

Side 1: 1. King of the Mountain (Stanley/Kulick/ Desmond Child) 4:17; 2. Any Way You Slice It (Simmons/Howard Rice) 4:02; 3. Who Wants to Be Lonely (Stanley/Child/Jean Beauvoir) 4:01; 4. Trial by Fire (Simmons/Kulick) 3:25; 5. I'm Alive (Stanley/Kulick/Child) 3:43.

Side 2: 1. Love's a Deadly Weapon (Simmons/ Stanley/Rod Swenson/Wes Beach) 3:29; 2. Tears Are Falling (Stanley) 3:55; 3. Secretly Cruel (Simmons) 3:41; 4. Radar for Love (Stanley/Child) 3:25; 5. Uh! All Night (Stanley/ Child/Beauvoir) 3:43.

Notes: Guitarist Bruce Kulick replaces Mark St. John.

CRAZY NIGHTS

Released on September 21, 1987; Mercury 422 832 626-1 Q-1.

Recorded March–June 1987 at Can-Am Recorders, Tarzana, CA; One on One, Hollywood, CA; and Rumbo Recorders, Los Angeles, CA.

Produced by Ron Nevison.

Side 1: 1. Crazy Crazy Nights (Stanley/Adam Mitchell) 3:45; 2. I'll Fight Hell to Hold You (Stanley/Mitchell/Kulick) 4:10; 3. Bang Bang You (Stanley/Desmond Child) 3:53; 4. No, No, No (Simmons/Kulick/Carr) 4:19; 5. Hell or High Water (Simmons/Kulick) 3:28; 6. My Way (Stanley/Child/Bruce Turgon) 3:58.

Side 2: 1. When Your Walls Come Down (Stanley/Mitchell/Kulick) 3:25; 2. Reason to Live (Stanley/Child) 3:59; 3. Good Girl Gone Bad (Simmons/Davitt Sigerson/Peter Diggins) 4:35; 4. Turn on the Night (Stanley/Dianne Warren) 3:19; 5. Thief in the Night (Simmons/Mitch Weissman) 4:05.

HOT IN THE SHADE

Released on October 17, 1989; Mercury 422 838 913-1 Q-1.

Recorded July–August 1989 at The Fortress, Hollywood, CA.

Produced by Gene Simmons and Paul Stanley.

Side 1: 1. Rise to It (Stanley/Bob Halligan Jr.) 4:08; 2. Betrayed (Simmons/Tommy Thayer) 3:38; 3. Hide Your Heart (Stanley/Desmond Child/Holly Knight) 4:25; 4. Prisoner of Love (Simmons/Bruce Kulick) 3:52; 5. Read My Body (Stanley/Halligan Jr.) 3:48; 6. Love's a Slap in the Face (Simmons/Vini Poncia) 4:04; 7. Forever (Stanley/Michael Bolton) 3:52; 8. Silver Spoon (Stanley/Poncia) 4:38.

Side 2: 1. Cadillac Dreams (Simmons/Poncia) 3:44; 2. King of Hearts (Stanley/Poncia) 4:26; 3. The Street Giveth and the Street Taketh Away (Simmons/Thayer) 3:34; 4. You Love Me to Hate You (Stanley/Child) 4:00; 5. Somewhere Between (Heaven and Hell) (Simmons/Poncia) 3:52; 6. Little Caesar (Carr/Simmons/Adam Mitchell) 3:08; 7. Boomerang (Simmons/Kulick) 3:30.

REVENGE

Released on May 19, 1992; Mercury 848 037-2.

Recorded February 1991–March 1992 at Rumbo Recorders, Track Records, Cornerstone, Ocean Way, Acme, and The Enterprise in Los Angeles, CA.

Produced by Bob Ezrin.

1. Unholy (Simmons/Vinnie Vincent) 3:40; 2. Take It Off (Stanley/Bob Ezrin/Kane Roberts) 4:50; 3. Tough Love (Stanley/Kulick/Ezrin) 3:44; 4. Spit (Simmons/Scott Van Zen/Stanley) 3:32; 5. God Gave Rock 'n' Roll to You II (Russ Ballard/Stanley/Simmons/Ezrin) 5:18; 6. Domino (Simmons) 4:01; 7. Heart of Chrome (Stanley/Vincent/Ezrin) 4:02; 8. Thou Shalt Not (Simmons/Jesse Damon) 3:59; 9. Every Time I Look at You (Stanley/Ezrin) 4:38; 10. Paralyzed (Simmons/Ezrin) 4:14; 11. I Just Wanna (Stanley/Vincent) 4:07; 12. Carr Jam 1981 (Carr) 2:46.

Notes: Drummer Eric Singer replaces Eric Carr.

CARNIVAL OF SOULS: THE FINAL SESSIONS

Released on October 28, 1997; Mercury 314 536 323-2.

Recorded November 1995–February 1996 at Music Grinder Studios, Hollywood, CA.

Coproduced by Toby Wright and Gene Simmons/Paul Stanley.

1. Hate (Simmons/Scott Van Zen/Kulick) 4:36; 2. Rain (Stanley/Kulick/Curtis Cuomo) 4:46; 3. Master & Slave (Stanley) 4:57; 4. Childhood's End (Simmons/Tommy Thayer/Kulick) 4:20; 5. I Will Be There (Stanley/Kulick/Cuomo) 3:49; 6. Jungle (Stanley/Kulick/Cuomo) 6:49; 7. In My Head (Simmons/Van Zen/Jaime St. James) 4:00; 8. It Never Goes Away (Stanley/Kulick/Cuomo) 5:42; 9. Seduction of the Innocent (Simmons/Van Zen) 5:16; 10. I Confess (Simmons/Ken Tamplin) 5:23; 11. In the Mirror (Stanley/Kulick/Cuomo) 4:26; 12. I Walk Alone (Simmons/Kulick) 6:07.

PSYCHO CIRCUS

Released on September 22, 1998; Mercury 314 558 992-2.

Recorded January–April 1998 at A&M Studios, Hollywood, CA, and One on One, New York, NY.

Produced by Bruce Fairbairn.

1. Psycho Circus (Stanley/Curtis Cuomo) 5:30; 2. Within (Simmons) 5:10; 3. I Pledge Allegiance to the State of Rock & Roll (Stanley/Cuomo/Holly Knight) 3:32; 4. Into the Void (Frehley/Karl Cochran) 4:22; 5. We Are One (Simmons) 4:41; 6. You Wanted the Best (Simmons) 4:15; 7. Raise Your Glasses (Stanley/Knight) 4:14; 8. I Finally Found My Way (Stanley/Bob Ezrin) 3:40; 9. Dreamin' (Stanley/Bruce Kulick) 4:12; 10. Journey of 1,000 Years (Simmons) 4:47.

Notes: Guitarist Ace Frehley replaces Bruce Kulick and drummer Peter Criss replaces Eric Singer.

SONIC BOOM

Released on October 6, 2009.

Recorded August 2007 and May–August 2009 at Conway, Henson Recording, and The Nook, Los Angeles, CA.

Produced by Paul Stanley; coproduced by Greg Collins.

1. Modern Day Delilah (Stanley) 3:37; 2. Russian Roulette (Simmons/Stanley) 4:32; 3. Never Enough (Stanley/Thayer) 3:26; 4. Yes I Know (Nobody's Perfect) (Simmons) 3:02; 5. Stand (Stanley/Simmons) 4:50; 6. Hot and Cold (Simmons) 3:36; 7. All for the Glory (Stanley/Simmons) 3:49; 8. Danger Us (Stanley) 4:22; 9. I'm an Animal (Stanley/Simmons/Thayer) 3:47; 10. When Lightning Strikes (Thayer/Stanley) 3:45; 11. Say Yeah (Stanley) 4:27.

Notes: The album includes a bonus disc of fifteen rerecorded "Kiss Klassics" as well as a bonus DVD of six songs recorded live in Buenos Aires, Argentina. Guitarist Tommy Thayer replaces Ace Frehley and drummer Eric Singer replaces Peter Criss.

MONSTER

Released on October 9, 2012.

Recorded on April 13, 2011–January 6, 2012, at Conway Studios, Henson Studios, and The Nook, Los Angeles, CA.

Produced by Paul Stanley; coproduced by Greg Collins.

1. Hell or Hallelujah (Stanley) 4:07; 2. Wall of Sound (Stanley/Thayer/Simmons) 2:55; 3. Freak (Stanley/Thayer) 3:35; 4. Back to the Stone Age (Simmons/Thayer/Stanley/Singer) 3:01; 5. Shout Mercy (Stanley/Thayer) 4:04; 6. Long Way Down (Stanley/Thayer) 3:51; 7. Eat Your Heart Out (Simmons) 4:06; 8. The Devil Is Me (Simmons/Stanley/Thayer) 3:40; 9. Outta This World (Thayer) 4:29; 10. All for the Love of Rock & Roll (Stanley) 3:21; 11. Take Me Down Below (Simmons/Stanley/Thayer) 3:24; 12. Last Chance (Stanley/Simmons/Thayer) 3:05.

SELECTED LIVE ALBUMS

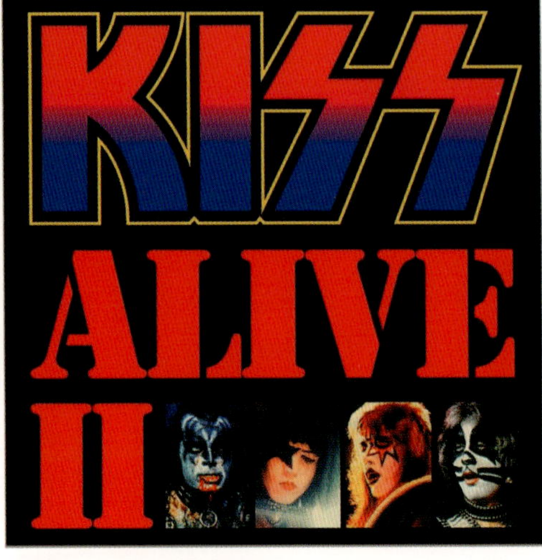

ALIVE!

Released on September 10, 1975; Casablanca NBLP 7020.

Recorded on May 16, 1975, at Cobo Arena, Detroit, MI; June 21, 1975, at Cleveland Music Hall, Cleveland, OH; July 20, 1975, at RKO Orpheum Theatre, Davenport, IA; July 23, 1975, at Wildwoods Convention Center, Wildwood, NJ.

Produced by Eddie Kramer.

Side 1: 1. Deuce; 2. Strutter; 3. Got to Choose; 4. Hotter Than Hell; 5. Firehouse.

Side 2: 1. Nothin' to Lose; 2. C'mon and Love Me; 3. Parasite; 4. She.

Side 3: 1. Watchin' You; 2. 100,000 Years; 3. Black Diamond.

Side 4: 1. Rock Bottom; 2. Cold Gin; 3. Rock and Roll All Nite; 4. Let Me Go, Rock 'n' Roll.

ALIVE II

Released on October 24, 1977; Casablanca NBLP 7076-2.

Recorded on April 2, 1977, at Budokan Hall, Tokyo, Japan; August 26–28, 1977, at The Forum, Los Angeles, CA; and September 13–16, 1977, at the Capitol Theatre, Passaic, NJ, and Electric Lady, New York, NY.

Produced by Kiss and Eddie Kramer.

Side 1: 1. Detroit Rock City; 2. King of the Night Time World; 3. Ladies Room; 4. Makin' Love; 5. Love Gun.

Side 2: 1. Calling Dr. Love; 2. Christine Sixteen; 3. Shock Me; 4. Hard Luck Woman; 5. Tomorrow and Tonight.

Side 3: 1. I Stole Your Love; 2. Beth; 3. God of Thunder; 4. I Want You; 5. Shout It Out Loud.

Side 4: 1. All American Man (Stanley/Sean Delaney) 3:12; 2. Rockin' in the USA (Simmons) 2:35; 3. Larger Than Life (Simmons) 3:58; 4. Rocket Ride (Frehley/Delaney) 4:06; 5. Any Way You Want It (Dave Clark) 2:53.

Notes: The "studio" side of new songs is a mix of in-studio work with live playing at the Capitol Theatre in Passaic. Additional guitars by Bob Kulick.

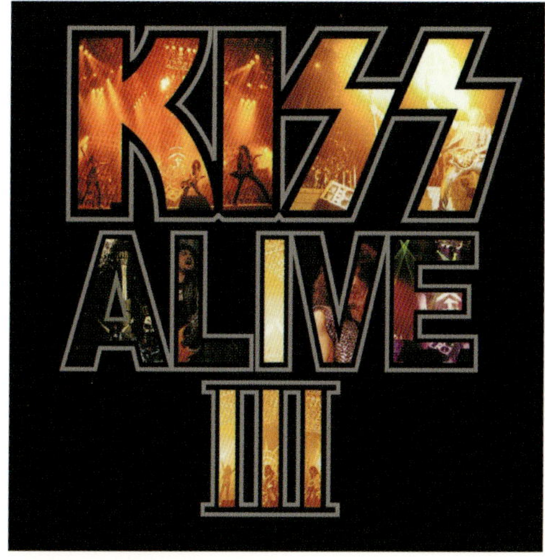

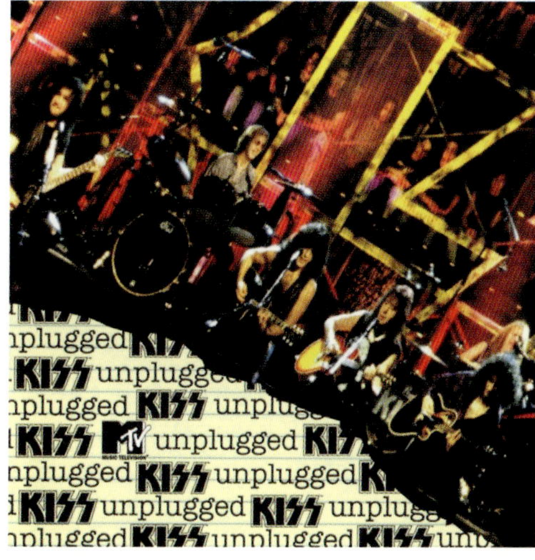

ALIVE III

Released on May 18, 1993; Mercury 314 514 777 2.

Recorded on November 27–29, 1992, at The Palace of Auburn Hills, Auburn Hills, MI; Market Square Arena, Indianapolis, IN; and Richfield Coliseum, Cleveland, OH.

Produced by Eddie Kramer and Kiss.

1. Creatures of the Night; 2. Deuce; 3. I Just Wanna; 4. Unholy; 5. Heaven's on Fire; 6. Watchin' You; 7. Domino; 8. I Was Made for Lovin' You; 9. I Still Love You; 10. Rock and Roll All Nite; 11. Lick It Up; 12. Forever; 13. I Love It Loud; 14. Detroit Rock City; 15. God Gave Rock 'n' Roll to You II; 16. Star Spangled Banner.

MTV UNPLUGGED

Released on March 12, 1996; Mercury 314 528 950-2.

Recorded on August 9, 1995, at Sony Studios, New York, NY.

Produced by Alex Coletti.

1. Comin' Home; 2. Plaster Caster; 3. Goin' Blind; 4. Do You Love Me; 5. Domino; 6. Sure Know Something; 7. A World Without Heroes; 8. Rock Bottom; 9. See You Tonite; 10. I Still Love You; 11. Every Time I Look at You; 12. 2000 Man; 13. Beth; 14. Nothin' to Lose; 15. Rock and Roll All Nite.

Notes: Acoustic live album, with cameos by Ace Frehley and Peter Criss.

SYMPHONY: ALIVE IV

Released on July 22, 2003; Sanctuary 06076-84624-2.

Recorded on February 28, 2003, at Telstra Dome, Melbourne, Australia.

Produced by Mark Opitz.

CD1: 1. Deuce; 2. Strutter; 3. Let Me Go, Rock 'n' Roll; 4. Lick It Up; 5. Calling Dr. Love; 6. Psycho Circus; 7. Beth; 8. Forever; 9. Goin' Blind; 10. Sure Know Something; 11. Shandi.

CD2: 1. Detroit Rock City; 2. King of the Night Time World; 3. Do You Love Me; 4. Shout It Out Loud; 5. God of Thunder; 6. Love Gun; 7. Black Diamond; 8. Great Expectations; 9. I Was Made for Lovin' You; 10. Rock and Roll All Nite.

Notes: Recorded live with the Melbourne Symphony Ensemble, Melbourne Symphony Orchestra, and as traditional four-man lineup consisting of Gene, Paul, Peter, and Tommy. Also issued as a single-CD package.

THE ORIGINALS

Released on July 21, 1976.

Notes: Lavish three-LP repackage of first three albums.

DOUBLE PLATINUM

Released on April 2, 1978.

Notes: First Kiss hits package, with many songs edited and remixed and "Strutter" re-recorded as "Strutter '78."

SMASHES, THRASHES & HITS

Released on November 15, 1988.

Notes: The band's second proper hits pack, and very successful at double platinum. Includes two previously unreleased tracks in "Let's Put the X in Sex" and "(You Make Me) Rock Hard." Also included is a rerecording of "Beth" with Eric Carr singing.

GREATEST KISS

Released on April 8, 1997.

Notes: Single CD compilation issued to capitalize on the reunion; almost went gold.

THE BOX SET

Released on November 20, 2001.

Notes: Lavish five-CD box set including many rarities.

THE VERY BEST OF

Released on August 27, 2002.

Notes: Gold-certified Mercury/UTV compilation; 21 tracks on a single CD.

THE 1978 SOLO ALBUMS

PAUL STANLEY

Released on September 18, 1978; Casablanca NBLP 7123.

Recorded February–July 1978 at Electric Lady and Record Plant, New York, NY, and The Village Recorder, Los Angeles, CA.

Produced by Paul Stanley and Jeff Glixman.

Side 1: 1. Tonight You Belong to Me (Stanley) 4:39; 2. Move On (Stanley/Mikel Japp) 3:07; 3. Ain't Quite Right (Stanley/Japp) 3:34; 4. Wouldn't You Like to Know Me (Stanley) 3:16; 5. Take Me Away (Together as One) (Stanley/Japp) 5:26.

Side 2: 1. It's All Right (Stanley) 3:31; 2. Hold Me, Touch Me (Stanley) 3:40; 3. Love in Chains (Stanley) 3:34; 4. Goodbye (Stanley) 4:09.

Notes: Paul also issued a solo album in 2006 called *Live to Win* and an album called *Now and Then* as leader of Paul Stanley's Soul Station.

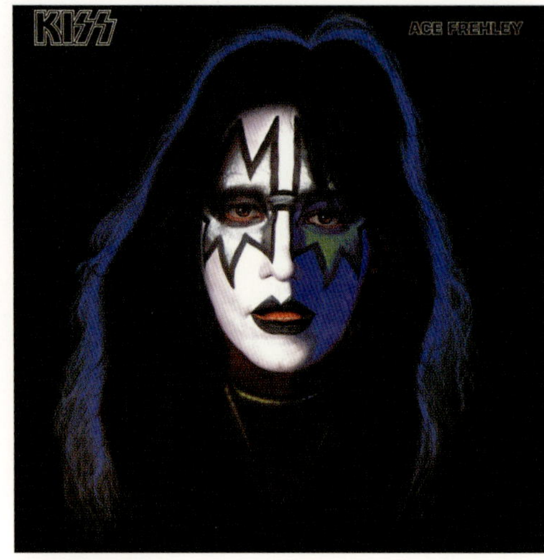

ACE FREHLEY

Released on September 18, 1978; Casablanca NBLP 7121.

Recorded June–July 1978 at The Mansion, Sharon, CT, and Plaza Sound Studios, New York, NY.

Produced by Eddie Kramer and Ace Frehley.

Side 1: 1. Rip It Out (Frehley/Larry Kelly/Sue Kelly) 3:39; 2. Speedin' Back to My Baby (Frehley/Jeanette Frehley) 3:35; 3. Snow Blind (Frehley) 3:54; 4. Ozone (Frehley) 4:36; 5. What's on Your Mind? (Frehley) 3:26.

Side 2: 1. New York Groove (Russ Ballard) 3:01; 2. I'm in Need of Love (Frehley) 4:36; 3. Wiped-Out (Frehley/Anton Fig) 4:10; Fractured Mirror (Frehley) 5:25.

Notes: Ace has an extensive solo catalog, following up this record with two Frehley's Comet albums, a self-titled and *Second Sighting,* and then *Trouble Walkin',* *Anomaly,* *Space Invader,* *Origins Vol. 1,* *Spaceman,* and *Origins Vol. 2.*

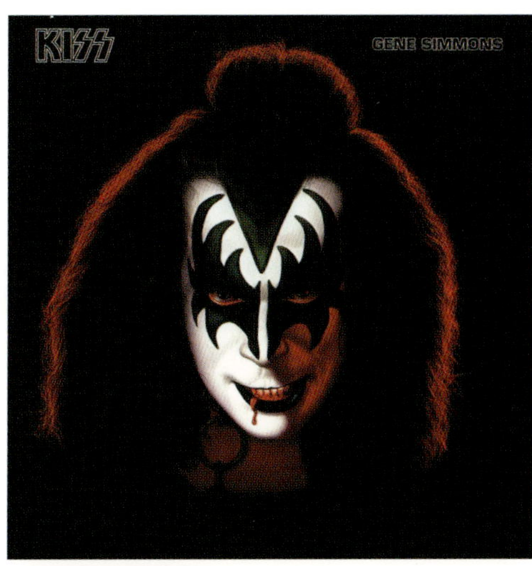

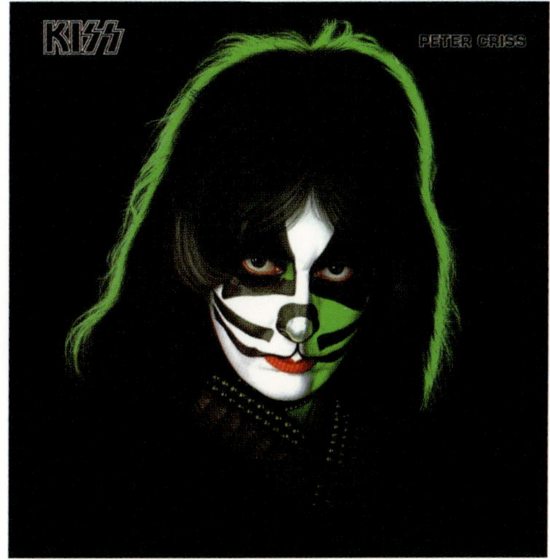

GENE SIMMONS

Released on September 18, 1978; Casablanca NBLP 7120.

Recorded April–July 1978 at The Manor, Oxfordshire, UK; Cherokee, Los Angeles, CA; and Blue Rock, New York, NY.

Produced by Sean Delaney and Gene Simmons.

Side 1: 1. Radioactive (Simmons) 3:52; 2. Burning Up with Fever (Simmons) 4:19; 3. See You Tonite (Simmons) 2:30; 4. Tunnel of Love (Simmons) 3:49; 5. True Confessions (Simmons) 3:30.

Side 2: 1. Living in Sin (Simmons/Sean Delaney/Howard Marks) 3:50; 2. Always Near You/Nowhere to Hide (Simmons) 4:12; 3. Man of 1000 Faces (Simmons) 3:16; 4. Mr. Make Believe (Simmons) 4:00; 5. See You in Your Dreams (Simmons) 2:48; 6. When You Wish Upon a Star (Ned Washington/Lee Harline) 2:44.

Notes: Gene also issued, in 2004, a solo album called *Asshole*.

PETER CRISS

Released on September 18, 1978; Casablanca NBLP 7122.

Recorded April–July 1978 at Electric Lady, New York, NY; Burbank Studios, Burbank, CA; and Sunset Sound, Hollywood, CA.

Produced by Vini Poncia.

Side 1: 1. I'm Gonna Love You (Criss/Stan Penridge) 3:18; 2. You Matter to Me (John Vastano/Michael Morgan/Vini Poncia) 3:15; 3. Tossin' and Turnin' (Ritchie Adams/Malou Rene) 3:58; 4. Don't You Let Me Down (Criss/Penridge) 3:38; 5. That's the Kind of Sugar Papa Likes (Criss/Penridge) 2:59.

Side 2: 1. Easy Thing (Criss/Penridge) 3:53; 2. Rock Me Baby (Sean Delaney) 2:50; 3. Kiss the Girl Goodbye (Criss/Penridge); 4. Hooked on Rock and Roll (Penridge/Criss/Poncia) 3:37; 5. I Can't Stop the Rain (Delaney) 4:25.

Notes: Peter was also part of Chelsea, which issued a self-titled album in 1970. As for solo work, Peter also issued *Out of Control* (1980), *Let Me Rock You* (1982), *Cat No. 1* (1994), and *One for All* (2007).

IMAGE CREDITS

A = all, B = bottom, C = center, L = left, M = main, R = right, T = top

Alamy Stock Photos: 26, Archive PL; 27, Media Punch; 29, Media Punch; 30, Media Punch; 31, Media Punch; 57M, Don Leavitt/Everett Collection; 80, Media Punch; 86R, Archive PL; 87M, ZUMA Press; 89M, Mirrorpix; 101T, dpa; 102–103, dpa; 105, JJs; 121M, dpa; 128 –129M, Bill Belknap; 133TR, RLFE Pix; 141, A7A Collection; 152, Album; 154R, ZUMA Press; 155, ZUMA Press; 159, Roberto Finizio/Alamy Live News; 161R, Sayre Berman; 163, Claudio Bresciani; 164–165, David Becker; 169, dpa; 170–171A, Media Punch; 172–173, ZUMA Press. **Robert Alford:** 12 –13A, 34–35A, 51M, 52T, 54T&B, 55TL, 55TR, 55BC, 65, 66T&B, 74–75A, 79M, 81M, 83R, 84M, 85M, 85R.

Associated Press: 21, Fryderyk Gabowicz/dpa; 127T, Wally Santana; 135, Associated Press; 138BL, Paul Spinelli/NFL Photos; 139, Mark Duncan; 144, David Callow; 145R, David Callow; 147M, Media Punch; 149–150A, Jae C Hong; 167, Andy Kropa/Invision. **Grant Ball Photography via Frank White Photo Agency:** 22–23A. Kevin Estrada: 115, 116–117, 123M, 148. **Getty Images:** 3, Fin Costello/Redferns; 5, Fin Costello/Redferns; 7, Michael Putland/Hulton Archive; 9, David Tan/Shinko Music/Hulton Archive; 10, Fin Costello/Redferns; 18,

Michael Putland/Hulton Archive; 24, Michael Ochs Archives; 33B, Tom Hill/WireImage; 37, Stephanie Maze/*San Francisco Chronicle*; 39B, Michael Ochs Archives; 41–45A, Fin Costello/Redferns; 47, Fin Costello/Redferns; 49, Fin Costello/Redferns; 52B, Fin Costello/Redferns; 53, Fin Costello/Redferns; 59T, Tom Hill/WireImage; 60–61, Tom Hill/WireImage; 70, Koh Hasebe/Shinko Music; 90, Lynn Goldsmith/Corbis Historical; 93M, Lynn Goldsmith/Corbis Historical; 95, Fin Costello/Redferns; 97, Mike Slaughter/*Toronto Star*; 98, Ebet Roberts/Redferns; 119, Ebet Roberts/Redferns; 124, Mick Hutson/Redferns; 127B, David Brewster/*Star Tribune*; 131, Pete Still/Redferns; 133M, David Lefranc/Sygma; 136, Brad Elterman/FilmMagic; 143, Liz Hafalia/*The San Francisco Chronicle*; 153, David Livingston; 160, John Kisch Archive; 161L, Lynn Goldsmith/Corbis Historical; 192, Fin Costello/Redferns. **ImaslevART:** 2, 4, 6, 8. **Photofest:** 63, 69M, 76M, 77R, 107. **Martin Popoff Collection:** 15A, 17, 33CT, 54BR, 67TL, 67BL, 69BL, 69BR, 83L, 84BL, 89BR, 91R, 103BR, 104TRBL, 104BR, 112R, 115TR, 118, 119R, 120R, 128L, 133TL. **Frank White via Frank White Photo Agency:** 109M, 110–111, 113B, 137.

ABOUT THE AUTHOR

At approximately 7,900 reviews (with more than 7,000 appearing in his books), Martin has unofficially written more record reviews than anybody in the history of music writing across all genres. In addition, Martin has penned approximately 115 books on hard rock, heavy metal, prog, punk, classic rock, and record collecting. He was editor in chief of the now retired *Brave Words & Bloody Knuckles*, Canada's foremost metal publication for fourteen years, and has also contributed to *Revolver, Guitar World, Goldmine, Record Collector*, bravewords.com, lollipop.com, and hardradio.com, with many record label band bios and liner notes to his credit as well. Martin has also been a regular contractor to Banger Films, having worked for two years as a researcher on the award-winning documentary *Rush: Beyond the Lighted Stage* and on the writing and research teams for the eleven-episode *Metal Evolution* and the ten-episode *Rock Icons,* both for VH1 Classic. In addition, Martin is the writer of the original heavy metal genre chart used in *Metal: A Headbanger's Journey* and throughout the *Metal Evolution* episodes. Martin currently resides in Toronto and can be reached at martinp@inforamp.net or through www.martinpopoff.com.

Quarto.com
© 2023 Quarto Publishing Group USA Inc.
Text © 2023 Martin Popoff

First Published in 2023 by Motorbooks,
an imprint of The Quarto Group,
100 Cummings Center, Suite 265-D,
Beverly, MA 01915, USA.
T (978) 282-9590 F (978) 283-2742

Motorbooks titles are also available at
discount for retail, wholesale, promotional,
and bulk purchase. For details, contact
the Special Sales Manager by email at
specialsales@quarto.com or by mail at The
Quarto Group, Attn: Special Sales Manager,
100 Cummings Center, Suite 265-D, Beverly,
MA 01915, USA.

27 26 25 24 23   1 2 3 4 5

ISBN: 978-0-7603-8182-3

Digital edition published in 2023
eISBN: 978-0-7603-8183-0

Library of Congress Cataloging-in-Publication
Data

Names: Popoff, Martin, 1963- author.
Title: Kiss @ 50 / Martin Popoff.
Other titles: Kiss at Fifty

Description: Beverly: Motorbooks, 2023. |
Includes index. | Summary: "Celebrate a
half-century of the hottest band in the land
with Kiss at 50, a handsome retrospective by
top metal journalist Martin Popoff featuring
rare photos, memorabilia, and a gatefold
timeline"-- Provided by publisher

Identifiers: LCCN 2023010305 | ISBN
9780760381823 | ISBN 9780760381830
 (ebook)
Subjects: LCSH: Kiss (Musical group)--
Anecdotes. | Rock musicians--United
 States--Anecdotes. | Rock music--United
States--History and criticism.
Classification: LCC ML421.K57 P67 2023 | DDC
 782.42166092/2--dc23/eng/20230308
LC record available at https://lccn.loc.
gov/2023010305

Design and layout: Burge Agency
Cover Image: Ginny Winn/Michael Ochs
Archives/Getty Images
Back cover image: Photofest

Printed in China

KISS

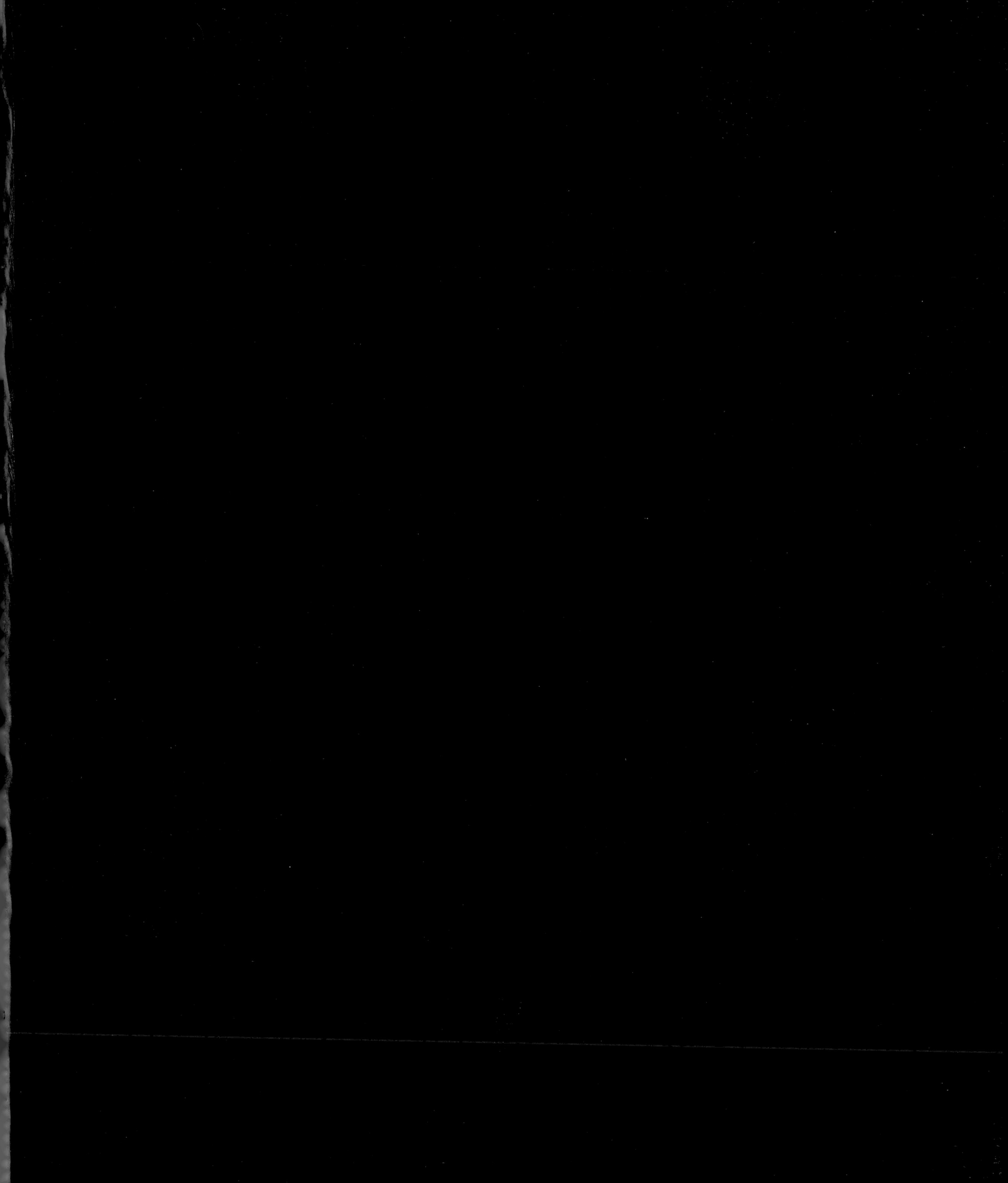